A DEEP
and
SUBTLE JOY

Life at Quarr Abbey

"I came that they may have life, and have it abundantly."
John 10:10

Luke Bell, OSB
with a Foreword by Tony Hendra

Map created by Ian Thomson, illustrator. Contact Information: it@imat3.fsnet. co.uk. Used with permission.

Unless otherwise noted, the scripture quotations outlined herein are from the Revised Standard Version Bible, New Testament, copyright 1946; Old Testament, copyright 1952; The Catholic Edition of the complete Bible incorporating Old Testament, New Testament and with the Apocrypha, copyright 1966. Published by the Catholic Truth Society, London. All rights reserved.

Cover design by Mary Belibasakis
Book design by Lynn Else

Library of Congress Cataloging-in-Publication Data

Bell, Luke.
    A deep and subtle joy : life at Quarr Abbey / Luke Bell ; with a foreword by Tony Hendra.
        p. cm.
    ISBN 1-58768-037-8 (alk. paper)
    1. Quar Abbey. 2. Isle of Wight (England)—Church history. I. Hendra, Tony. II. Title.
    BX2596.Q37B45 2006
    271'.104228—dc22

                                                                    2006013228

Published by
HiddenSpring
An imprint of Paulist Press
997 Macarthur Boulevard
Mahwah, New Jersey, 07430

www.hiddenspringbooks.com

Printed and bound in the United States of America

For my goddaughter Hannah

ACKNOWLEDGMENT

The author and publisher wish to express their gratitude to Sister Mary Totah, OSB, and St. Cecilia's Abbey (Ryde, Isle of Wight, PO33 1LH) for permission to use copyright material from *The Spirit of Solesmes,* published in 1997 by Burns & Oates, Wellwood, North Farm Road, Tunbridge Wells, Kent TN2 3DR, United Kingdom, and by St. Bede's Publications, P.O. Box 545, 271 N. Main Street, Petersham, MA 01366-0545, USA.

Quarr Abbey, RYDE, Isle of Wight, PO33 4ES, United Kingdom
www.quarrabbey.co.uk
www.stceciliasabbey.org.uk

CONTENTS

FOREWORD

Long ago and far away, when I was not much more than a boy, I found a magical place, a secret garden, my private Eden, my personal Narnia. In victorious post-war England, a dark and depressive land where one was raised to be skeptical and gritty and have few expectations, magic was a suspect commodity. I knew this and was careful to keep my discovery secret as long as possible, but I also felt a guilty pleasure in having found somewhere I could immerse myself without reserve. Here was a place of beauty to which I could give my whole being—not look at it askance and wonder in what way it would betray me, the way the sunlit dream of England and empire had betrayed my parents and grandparents. It was a place out of time, out of England—literally, on a little island off its south coast called the Isle of Wight—but in another quite different sense it was a fore-taste of eternity, an *amuse-bouche* of paradise.

Its name was Quarr Abbey—the Abbey in which this exquisite little book unfolds.

The timeless physical beauty of Quarr, its breathtaking completeness, the neatly ordered farm and fields beside a wild and always whitecapped sea was not the first thing about it I met and knew. Before that I met a monk, whom I had expected to be what I feared most in my religion: the dark, faceless hood of retribution, a spine-chilling gothic figure gliding down murky stone stairs or along an echoing cloister, to get me. A monk was the ultimate nightmare of a boy who'd sinned—and hadn't we all sinned big-time?—in the unforgiving world of pre–Vatican II Catholicism.

What I found instead was a warm and forgiving friend, a man who never failed to bring a smile to my lips the moment I set eyes on him, who laid the foundations of my self and personality, who never gave up on me through all the apostasies of my life—until decades later, there he was, my spiritual father, waiting at the big oak door of the Abbey guest house for his prodigal son to come home.

His name was Father Joseph Warrilow, OSB, but everyone—including me—called him Father Joe.

Father Joe was a monk for seventy of his eighty-nine years, the majority of them spent at Quarr. From him I learned more than I can enumerate about spirituality, self-analysis and self-examination, literature, music, art, growing up, all things French...The list is without end. For the longest years of my life—my teens—I wanted passionately to become a Benedictine just like him, and learned much about specifically monastic matters, such as Gregorian chant, the Rule of Saint Benedict, and the profound influence of the Benedictines on the history and evolution of Europe. But beneath all this knowledge, and the relationship with Father Joe from which it sprang, was a deeper perception that framed it in larger terms. For the first time in my young life I had come face to face with tradition, tradition that lived in every note of the chant, every act of every monk, every psalm sung, every meal taken, every minute of work done, as it had done in much the same way in innumerable other communities stretching back for almost 1500 years.

For me it was Gregorian chant that evoked the Benedictine tradition most vividly. I found it thrilling that had I been able to visit a Benedictine house a thousand years earlier, I would have heard the same exquisite Latin hymns sung at Compline as I did at Quarr before the community retired for the night. And although Quarr was not that old a foundation and its buildings were not much more than fifty years old at the time, the sense of history they exuded was so deep as to be frightening—as if one was peeping over the rim of a gigantic chasm, so fathomless that the bottom was a complete mystery; except that somewhere down there, far away and far below, hidden in the dense shadows of time, stood a man called Benedict.

Father Joe once said to me a startling thing apropos the profound tradition from which he came. I had been singing praises about his uniqueness, his inimitable ability to listen and understand, and he demurred: "No, Tony dear. I'm just another old monk. There isn't a man here who wouldn't say the same things I do..."

It wasn't until many years later that I came to understand that this wasn't just humility. He really meant that he was just another Benedictine. However incomparable his wisdom and understanding, they didn't belong to him but to the tradition that had shaped and nurtured him. Down through all those centuries and communities there had been other Father Joes, known and unknown, helping and understanding and listening to lost and imperfect and troubled souls.

There is an important counterpart to Benedictine tradition, however, one just as profoundly Benedictine.

After he died in 1998, I wrote a book about Father Joe, which came out in 2004. It was an election year and inevitably at readings and panels, someone would ask the not terribly productive question: who would Father Joe have voted for? I would usually evade the question with some flippant answer, but it did set me thinking about what it was that had attracted me to him and to Quarr when we first met in the mid-50s.

After all I had been raised by a Labor-Party working-class father to be a good little socialist. All my young instincts and received wisdom were inimical to tradition. The past was where terrible social injustices had spawned and multiplied; tradition summed up the dead hand of class and privilege. One of these fine revolutionary days, we would wipe both off the map forever. And yet here I was at the age of fifteen, thrilling to tradition, being swept up by it every time the ancient, ethereal music of the chant filled my ears. Was I a closet conservative?

But I was also deeply attracted to the Benedictines' rejection of the world and their embrace of poverty. The idea of being free—not just of possessions but of the need to acquire and own things—was as thrilling to me as the chant. And in a modern, money-driven, consumerist society, what could be more subversive, more revolutionary, than to reject the very act of consuming?

I came to see that the Benedictine way of life could not be pigeonholed politically, however passionately partisan you might be. The choice that each man made in embracing his lifelong vows was at once profoundly conservative and profoundly revolutionary. This rock-solid spiritual equilibrium, I have always thought, is one of the secrets of the Benedictines' extraordinary longevity.

Father Luke's book demonstrates and celebrates another aspect of the subversive, one very different from the vow of poverty but connected to it. When a man or woman makes the decision to become a contemplative, she or he doesn't just leave one world behind. In devoting themselves to God they discover an entirely new world—a world seen with new eyes; an intensely present world; every detail of it, however humble or mundane, bristling with the meaning and nature and purpose of our existence. Father Luke's method underlines gently but memorably something Father Joe never tired of repeating to me over the years in a hundred different ways: the ordinary is the divine and the divine ordinary. The divine is everywhere. It's just as much in the smell of the hay or the faces on the bus or the petals of a daisy as it is in the majesty of the mountains or the tranquility of a cathedral.

And nothing, of course, is more ordinary than work—and in the world more tedious, more exploitative, more rule-ridden, more restricting and enslaving. But in the monastery it becomes the very opposite of these things—liberating, uplifting, a means of contact with the divine. *Laborare est orare,* "to work is to pray," is one of the best known of all Benedictine *dicta* and one that for me has always summed up the combination of common sense and striving for sanctity that made Saint Benedict unique in history and his Rule the one that survived all others.

Much of the history of monasticism, from the mind-boggling asceticism of the desert fathers to the ferocious self-mortification of sixteenth-century Carmelites, stresses negation of body, suppression of human needs and feelings, and complete detachment from the world and the ordinary fabric of life. You could say that it comes down decisively on the sanctity side of the equation, the divine side, at the expense of the commonsense and ordinary. But Saint Benedict's way is a gentler, more tolerant, and more inclusive one, which is not to say lax—for obedience, and the discipline that flows from it, is still the glue of monastic life. Rather, Benedict's way makes allowances for human weakness and venality, for the myriad temperaments in a community, the untidiness and lumpiness of life.

One of my favorite parts of the Rule is where Saint Benedict says with perhaps a certain resignation: "Since we cannot prevail upon our brothers not to drink, let us at least take wine in moderation." He goes on to detail how much that might be. While many would-be saints take an all-or-nothing attitude to their search for perfection, for Saint Benedict there is a lot of room between all and nothing.

So many of Father Luke's musings bring Quarr back to life for me; for example, his meditation on the great trees of Quarr. As it does for him now, fifty years ago it was the great oaks of Quarr that best symbolized for me its rootedness, its striving, and its strength. There is something about the knotty bark of the oaks' thick trunks and branches that reminded me literally of massive limbs. I would imagine I could see huge muscles and sinews flexing with infinite slowness beneath that rough skin.

The most magical moment I remember at Quarr was one bright spring morning, fifty years gone, when I was fifteen. An old French lay brother called Frere Louis and I had been sent to work in Quarr's oak woods after morning Mass, to clear brush between the mighty trees. There were bluebells everywhere and a dazzling light—for the oak leaves were not yet fully formed—and as we moved slowly through the woods, in total silence except for our hatchets clanging through the saplings, I understood completely how work could be prayer, how doing a simple job, immersed in a green throbbing buzzing shining welter of life, could bring you into direct contact with the God who lives in every atom of existence.

Many details of Father Luke's tour of Quarr stay with me, in part because they are familiar Benedictine themes. For example, his insight that the trimming and training of trees is a perfect metaphor for how the obedience and discipline of the monastic community shape its individual members.

I remember very much the same insight long ago on another day when I had been recruited to help "lay" a hawthorn hedge. A largely lost art, hedge-laying involves cutting into and splitting (but not severing) the branches of individual hawthorn bushes, then bending and weaving them so that they grow together to become one strong, continuous, and impenetrable hedge. Here, I thought, was an apt metaphor for how the community was formed, the cutting and bending and weaving that had to be done for the human hawthorns to blend together into one solid living thing. With skill and care, well-laid hedges would survive for centuries; so would a properly trained community.

One more great Benedictine principle—perhaps the most subtle and paradoxical—is that the only way to find your true self is to lose it in the community, to drown in the river of tradition, music, liturgy, routine, work, and obedience, so that you emerge selfless but fully realized as the person God first and last wanted you to be. This book has that great and ancient principle at its core; its simplicity is not superficiality, but quite the opposite: a stripping away of all that is unnecessary in our lives—and so much of it is—in order to concentrate our energies on the contemplation and experience of the divine.

What the Benedictines can teach lay people whose vocations are in marriage and parenthood and innumerable areas of social involvement—healthcare, teaching, technical and intellectual skills are just a few—is that it isn't necessary to become a contemplative in order to live in the world but not of it. We can achieve the same sense of community, the same goal of selflessness and service to others, by perceiving in the simplest of our actions, the most mundane details of our quotidian lives, opportunities to greet God. And thus to find in the world what Father Joe and Father Luke and countless others found in the ineffable tranquility of the monastic life: a deep and subtle joy.

Tony Hendra, author of
Father Joe: The Man Who Saved My Soul

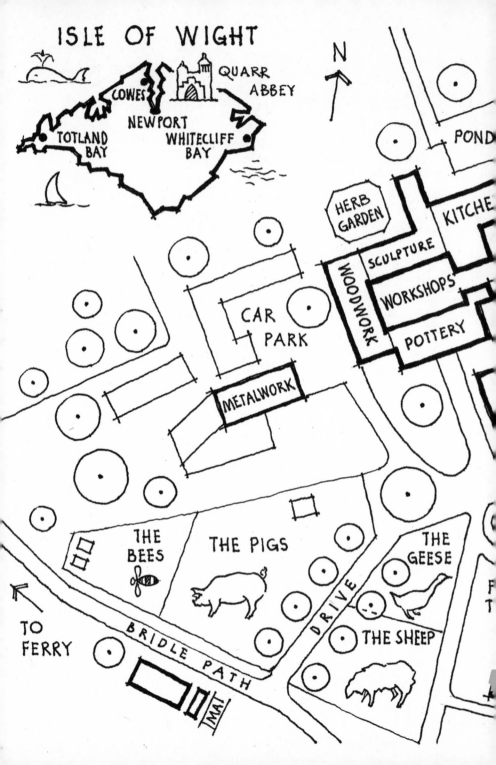

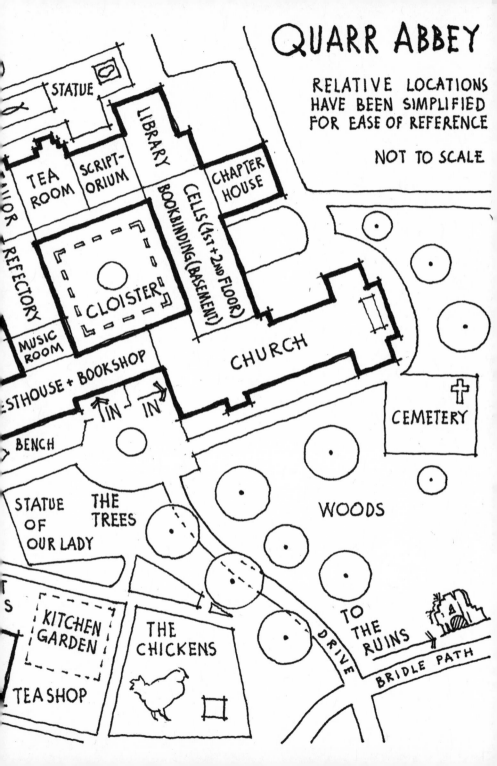

INTRODUCTION

Quarr Abbey is a Benedictine monastery on the Isle of Wight. It is my home and, for me, a place of deep and subtle joy. I invite you to share this joy by spending twenty-four hours with me in this place. Through this book, I want to show you the various places in the monastery where we monks spend our lives, and to introduce you to the rhythm of our day. In doing so I want to tell you about some of the personal experiences that brought me here and to explain something of what this place and our life here mean to us.

This explanation will draw on two books. The first is the book of nature, which is full of spiritual meanings, speaking as it does of its Maker, "for from the greatness and beauty of created things comes a corresponding perception of their Creator."[1] The second is the Bible. These books, having the same Author, speak with one voice. Our life brings us into close contact with both. The care of our grounds, our livestock, and our crops allow nature to speak to us. We are privileged to live in a place of natural beauty, where we only have to step out of the door to enjoy the woods, the flowers, the birds, and the sea. Our daily pondering of the scriptures allows God's written word to speak to us. At the heart of our lives is our worship in the church, the staple food of which is the psalms. The psalms therefore naturally furnish many of the scriptural illustrations of this book's themes.

Our life is concerned with seeking to allow God to draw closer to us. He is our joy. To share our life with you is to share our search for him. Our search happens in a particular place and

---

1. Wisdom 13:5

with a particular use of time. This is why this book describes various areas in the monastery and particular moments in the day. The former give each chapter its title, but there is also a spiritual theme in every chapter and this is indicated by its subtitle. The chapters are organized according to the rhythm of the day.

I hope you will come to share our love for this place and its rhythm. And I pray that you, in your own place and your own time, will know the joy of God.

QUARR ABBEY TIMETABLE

5:30 a.m.
Vigils

7:00 a.m.
Lauds, followed by spiritual reading

9:00 a.m.
Mass

10:15 a.m.
Morning work

1:00 p.m.
Sext, followed by lunch and community recreation

2:20 p.m.
None, followed by afternoon work

4:30 p.m.
Tea

5:00 p.m.
Vespers

7:00 p.m.
Supper

8:30 p.m.
Compline, followed by night silence

Chapter One

THE ISLE OF WIGHT

Recollections of Childhood and Intimations of Eternity

Holiness is our goal in the monastery. In all our labors, whether they are outdoors for the husbandry of our land or inside in the silence of our cells seeking to allow God to speak to us through sacred texts, we are working toward holiness. Holiness is being fully open to the joy of God. Man is made for holiness. Although this may be forgotten, there is often still a sense that holidays are important. Once these were, precisely, *holy* days. And even now a holiday may be a way for people to see a little beyond their work among the things of this world: a time apart, in a place apart.

The Isle of Wight is for me a holiday place. It is full of childhood memories of holidays. My family came first to the east of the island, from Ryde on the steam train to Shanklin. I don't remember much about it other than the sand sticking to the cream put on my sunburn! But I remember well our trips to Whitecliff Bay. We sent luggage in advance, which went on the train to Brading Station. Our home for the holiday was a little wooden house just outside what is now a trailer park. It had an outside chemical toilet, which had to be emptied by carrying the contents up the hill to the sewage tank. Down the path from the little house was the sea. When the tide was out, it was possible to

1

walk a bit along the foot of Culver Cliff. Up the path from the house was the top of Culver Cliff. From this it was possible to walk down to Sandown Zoo. Going along the top from the house in the opposite direction, we came to Bembridge and the Crab & Lobster, where my father bought my brother and me peanuts.

Here I knew what it was to be a child. I remember saying to my mother here, "I love you." Now I am again on the Isle of Wight. My parents are no longer alive, but I am living in an abbey dedicated to the Mother of all Christians, whom I also love. I am trying to live again as a child, a child of the Eternal Father. Jesus said, "Whoever does not receive the kingdom of God like a child shall not enter it."[1] So I seek to follow the Lord's words and have a childlike trust, to take each moment as it comes as a special gift of God's providence. In Whitecliff Bay, I would imagine what I might do in the future, such as making a film of the zoo. Now, not far short of half a century later, my mind sometimes turns more readily to the past. But I seek to train it to remember eternity, to dwell on (and by an anticipated participation, in) our heavenly homeland, Jerusalem the Golden.

Some years ago I revisited that little wooden house. It was wrecked. Coats of paint put on long after we had stopped going there were peeling away from the worn and disintegrating timbers. There was only rusty junk in the bedroom where my brother and I had once slept. Where once the chemical toilet had been was a modern flush toilet, now smashed and abandoned. Yet standing there, looking at the ruined house, my feeling was that I was once again a little child, on holiday with my brother, my mother and father, and my grandmother. I felt, as a child does, wonder and joy. I was once more on a childhood holiday. At the same moment, I knew—the evidence was all before me—that this time was passing. It did not have enduring existence. It could not last, any more

---

1. Mark 10:15

than the little house could last. And suspended between time past and time present, I glimpsed what is beyond all time. I had an intuition of eternity, from which our moments of childhood and our moments of maturity have their being. I knew that this is the only enduring reality. Everything else is relative to it and, like that house, not enduring. If any of the moments of our life speak to our heart, they speak of this eternity.

I have been back to the site since then. The little house is no longer there at all. There is only the concrete foundation on which it once stood. But the eternity of which my boyhood was a reflection, the eternity that I glimpsed as that time past once more touched my heart: that eternity is the goal of my life as I live it now on this very special island.

My early childhood memories are of Whitecliff Bay, but my later childhood holidays were spent in Totland Bay on the west side of the island. From there we walked over Headon Warren to Alum Bay, where in those days you could fill glass-model light-houses with colored sands from the bay. From Alum Bay we walked over Tennyson Down, named after the poet who so much enjoyed walking there, with its fine commanding views. But these were only activities for cooler days. When the weather was warm, which was most of the time, we sat on the beach, a bit away from where most people were. We would look out across the Solent, which is a strait of the English Channel, toward Hurst Point, a castellated structure built by Henry the Eighth for defensive purposes. We would watch the boats go past. One time we made a special point of observing a ferry taking our aunt, uncle, and cousins to France. I would make fires on the beach and go for swims in the sea. That little fragment of the coast became our daytime holiday home. Year after year we came back to it, and it became an enduring presence in our hearts.

Decades later, after I had come to Quarr Abbey as a monk, I went on a cruise with some other monks by the kindness of the owner of a very fine motor cruiser boat. We made our way gently out of Cowes, and when we reached the open sea, the owner turned on the power and in about twenty minutes we reached Hurst Point, which I had sat contemplating across the water so many times all those years ago. After a chance to see some seabirds and eat a light lunch, we went along the coast of the mainland until the Needles—the imposing rocks by Alum Bay that form the western tip of the island—were due south. We turned in that direction and went swiftly toward them. I had never seen them so close-up or sharply in focus. You could see every bird sitting on top of them. Then we came back along the coast of West Wight. Alum Bay looked particularly beautiful. The low but bright sun was shining on the different colored sands to reveal them in a splendor never seen in a glass lighthouse. As we cruised back past Headon Warren and Totland Bay, I had the sensation not so much of revisiting the past as of *being* in the past and seeing it in an extraordinary dimension that at the time was unimagined. We spent so long looking out from the shore, but I had never looked *into* it—or visited Hurst point—before.

That experience of seeing a hidden dimension in time spoke of what we are about in the monastery. Each moment contains a vista of eternity. Just as I did not know, as I sat on the beach, how we appeared from out there on the open sea, so most of the time we do not know what the moments of our life are when viewed from the boundless ocean of eternity. In the monastery we try to live with an understanding, given to us by faith and sometimes by intuition, of what our moments look like from eternity. We aim to treasure the richness of eternal life hidden in our time here.

Coming back from that cruise on the Solent, we went into the church to sing Vespers, and as we came out after the service the moon was shining brightly on the cloister, illuminating one of the gray slate roofs. So does eternity, the reflection of divine being, light up the ordinariness of our lives.

Whitecliff Bay and Totland Bay: these are the two places that mark my childhood memories of the island. Between them is the abbey where I now live. Here my life as a child is finding its fullness, from him who came that we might have life and have it abundantly.[2] Here I hope to live out my days, and to treasure each of them as one of the wrappings of eternity.

The Isle of Wight is a place apart, separated by the Solent from the rest of Britain. To come here as a child on holiday was always to come somewhere special, somewhere apart from our ordinary lives. The two weeks on the island were golden weeks, looked forward to and remembered long after. They were weeks when the whole family could be together. Quarr Abbey also is a place apart, a special place, and our time here is golden time, an anticipation of Jerusalem the Golden, our eternal home. We live in the monastic tradition of separation from the world. The sun shining golden on the red Belgium brick from which the monastery and its church are made speaks obscurely of a beauty beyond this world, the beauty of its very Creator who is the Light of Heaven. We seek to live from that light, living together as a family. And if there is in our life together a degree of apartness from others, it is only so as to be close to the One in whom there is no distance, the One in whom all have their being, the One in whom nobody is neglected, the One who is Love Itself.

And you can visit us. Come now, and let me show you the abbey.

---

2. John 10:10

Chapter Two

THE TREES

Spiritual Growth and How It Happens

Growing by the side of the main drive of the abbey are trees, pollarded in the French style. On either side, beyond the trees, are fields, sometimes with ponies in them. Come down this drive with me. I invite you to be my companion on this tour of Quarr Abbey, my home. Perhaps I can be a companion to you on your journey of life, too, wherever that takes you.

Halfway down the drive we cross a bridle way, which is designated for development as a bicycle path. If you were to go east down this, you would reach the ruins of Old Quarr, the medieval Cistercian monastery adjacent to which the present monastery was built. We'll visit it later in your time here. If you were to go west down the bridle way, you would reach the car ferry. In the days when I came as a guest, I used to walk up from the car ferry and then turn down the other drive, which turns off the bridle way west of this one. We'll take a look at what is there later too. First let us continue down the main drive beyond the bridle way. On our left is an orchard and beyond that to the west a walled garden in which there are more fruit trees. On the left side of the drive there is a grassy area. I remember one time when I was staying as a guest working here with an old French monk, scything the grass. He taught me that the rhythm is the important thing.

This is true of the Benedictine life, as well as of scything. It has its rhythm. Over this twenty-four hours that you are spending here, I hope you come to appreciate this rhythm. It is made up of interwoven times of prayer, reading, work, and recreation. Through this rhythm we aim to grow in our spiritual lives, to grow in holiness. Normally speaking, it is a slow growth, like that of a tree.

There is a tree here in the grass to the side of the drive beyond the orchard that for me is a perfect symbol of what we hope to become by growing. The tree, as one of the brothers remarked to me, has probably been here long before the present community of monks came. It speaks to me of one of the monks of Old Quarr. Toward the bottom of the trunk are marks where branches have been lopped off. These are, as it were, the obediences given to the monk by his abbot so that he could grow toward heaven. The monk accepted what his abbot asked of him, rather than do what he chose, so as to become more unselfish, more open to God. The missing branches are the things of his own choosing that he forwent to do what was asked of him. At the top of the tree, which is not far short of the height of the church, is a considerable expanse of evergreen foliage, speaking of the monk's openness to the light of heaven that his unselfishness made possible. He did the will of God, as expressed by his abbot's commands, and now he is close to heaven, where God's will is supreme.

I remember contemplating this tree while standing beneath the branches of another tree that I was pruning in the orchard on the other side of the wall. Against the background of a blue sky, I saw a rainbow arching over the tree and the church. It seemed like a visible manifestation of the peace whose spiritual presence pervades this place and this life, a peace that the world cannot give. The blue sky spoke of Mary, Queen of Peace, to whom the abbey is dedicated.

In the church, when we are remembering in our worship monks or nuns who have achieved that peace in their souls and are now saints in heaven, we sing a hymn that apostrophizes them as "lofty spreading cedar trees." It describes us who sing it as saplings by contrast with those who have gone before us. Trees, firmly rooted and reaching toward heaven, are a symbol of spiritual growth and resilience. We want to be like them. One of the psalms that we sing tells us how. It is the first in the psalter, and it lays out the program of the spiritual life. "Blessed is the man," it says, "who walks not in the counsel of the wicked, nor stands in the way of sinners, nor sits in the seat of scoffers; but his delight is in the law of the LORD, and on his law he meditates day and night."[1] The monk aims to be like this, seeking God's will and pondering the scriptures. "He is like," the psalm continues, "a tree planted by streams of water, that yields its fruit in its season, and its leaf does not wither."[2] Because of the water, the tree can cope with heat and with drought. Such is the one who is rooted through trust in the divine goodness, which he drinks in through prayer. Continually renewed by the sap of the Holy Spirit, his goodness does not wither in times of aridity and adversity. A monk seeks to pray continually so as to have this Spirit always in his heart.

The foundation of that prayer is trust. In words similar to those of the psalm, the prophet Jeremiah guides us to see this trust as the roots of a tree:

> Blessed is the man who trusts in the LORD,
>   whose trust is the LORD.
> He is like a tree planted by water,
>   that sends out its roots by the stream,
> and does not fear when heat comes,
>   for its leaves remain green,

1. Psalm 1:1–2
2. Psalm 1:3

and is not anxious in the year of drought,
  for it does not cease to bear fruit.[3]

The roots are the depth of the monk's relationship with God. On the surface things may be dry, but deep down the soul is being nourished by the Holy Spirit. The monk's spiritual life continues whatever the season. Aridity does not impede his relationship with God.

In the Bible (which we read often in the monastery), the tree symbolizes not only one who is living a spiritual life but also the very source of that life itself. At the beginning of the Bible, the Book of Genesis tells us of the tree of life in the midst of the garden of Eden[4] and at the end of the Bible, the Book of Revelation speaks again of "the tree of life with its twelve kinds of fruit, yielding its fruit each month," and says, "The leaves of the tree were for the healing of the nations."[5] According to an ancient tradition the Lord Jesus Christ himself is the tree of life. This identification is established through an interpretation of a saying of the Lord in St. Luke's Gospel. As Jesus is being led to his execution, he says, "If they do this when the wood is green, what will happen when it is dry?"[6] He is the one who is fully rooted in the Father, whom he trusts absolutely, and he is asking how people who do not have this trust can hope to cope with the onslaught of evil when they have no roots, no sap, no greenness. He shows us the way to trust. If a monk is seeking to be like a tree growing up to heaven, he is seeking to be like the Lord Jesus.

This great tree growing up to heaven is very different from the apple trees in the orchard next to it, but they too tell us about growing in holiness: by the fruit they bear. That fruit is a symbol

---

3. Jeremiah 17:7–8
4. Genesis 2:9
5. Revelation 22:2
6. Luke 23:31

of holiness, the only fruit of a human life that lasts. I'm not sure all the trees here produce fruit. At the end of this little bit of orchard by the drive there is one with diseased and dead wood. When I was pruning the trees, I considered just chopping it down, but then I thought it might yet produce some apples, so I left it for another year. I gave it one last chance. In a gospel parable, Jesus says it's the same for us.[7] We are being left so as to have the chance of producing fruit, the fruit of holiness. Of course, we don't expect to become holy overnight. That would be like going out into the orchard in the spring when the blossom is still on the fruit trees and expecting to be able to pick the fruit at once. Autumn is the time for fruit, and we look to reach holiness in the years of our maturity.

God, the All Holy One, is the source of holiness. We find holiness by seeking God. The Rule of St. Benedict, the monks' guide given to us by our father in faith, tells us this is what we should be doing.[8]

If we are seeking someone, it is helpful to have some idea of whom we are looking for. The Book of Exodus has a word for us about who God is. It narrates how God, speaking from a burning bush, commissions Moses to bring deliverance to his people. Moses is to announce this to the people and so he asks to know God's name. It is, he is told, "I AM WHO I AM."[9] This speaks of transcendent being. God is the one who has being in himself. He is the source of being. Relative to him, all created things are insubstantial: they have only relative being. St. Gregory the Great, a pope who wrote the life of St. Benedict, helps us to understand this in the account he gives of that holy man's vision of the world illumined by a single ray of divine light. It looks very small indeed and St. Gregory comments that to the soul seeking the

---

7. Luke 13:6–9
8. Chapter 58
9. Exodus 3:14

Creator, all creation is narrow.[10] The relation of the creation to the Creator is described by Meister Eckhart, the medieval mystic, as being like that of paint on a wall. The substance is all in God. Creation does not so much have being as give color to being.

We monks make that absolute being our goal. In seeking God we are seeking absolute being, the all-encompassing, not the narrow; the substance, not the color. Our priority is to be focused on this. That is why our declarations (the guidelines for our monastic congregation) say, "No activity is to become the purpose of our life, not even its secondary purpose, to the extent of modifying its essential conditions."[11] A monastery that does not follow this is even to be expelled from the congregation, so important is it for us not to be distracted by anything from focusing on absolute being.[12] Not even the worship in church qualifies to take the place of God's transcendent being.

The question arises of how we relate to the absolute being of the One Who Is, since his transcendence would seem to put him out of our reach. There is a clue to the answer in another monastery, an older one than this. St. Catherine's Monastery at the foot of Mount Sinai (now in Egypt) is on the site where Moses is traditionally supposed to have had his vision of the immanent Lord, as related in the Book of Exodus. For seventeen centuries this monastery has enjoyed an extraordinary providential protection by every ruling power in the area, including Napoleon Bonaparte. Hosni Mubarak, Egypt's president, and his wife have been there. This providential protection means that the tradition has been kept intact. Actually, on the site is even a bush that is supposed to be *the* bush. (I'm sorry we haven't got anything like that here I can show you!) In St. Catherine's one can also see very

---

10. *Dialogues,* Book Two, Chapter 35

11. Declarations for the Monasteries of Monks of the Solesmes Congregation, paragraph 31

12. Ibid., paragraph 35

ancient and beautiful holy icons. One of them is of the Blessed Virgin of the Burning Bush, an identification also made in our liturgy in the Christmas season.

This links Jesus to the "I AM WHO I AM" spoken from the burning bush. This identification is clear in St. John's Gospel where Jesus repeatedly uses the phrase *I Am,* for example, "I am the bread which came down from heaven,"[13] "I am the light of the world,"[14] "I am the resurrection and the life,"[15] "I am the way, and the truth, and the life,"[16] and "I am the true vine."[17] When they come to arrest him, he simply says (in the original Greek text), "I Am," and they fall to the ground, overcome by absolute being.[18]

So it is in Jesus that we receive the fullness of being and holiness. He is "the way, and the truth, and the life."[19] In his own person he shows us the God of truth whom we are to trust, and by trusting him in this way we find life. Through him we find absolute being. Just as the leaves of the tree of life are for healing, so we are made whole by him, the One who has taken our humanity into heaven. Our lives as monks are designed to be centered on him. In our daily celebration of Mass (which will be included in our tour of the Abbey tomorrow morning), we unite ourselves with him through communion. In our reading of the Gospels, both in public and in private, we ponder his words. In our personal prayer we use his name. It is at the center of the "Hail Mary," the most often-repeated prayer of the Rosary, and it is in that favorite prayer of the monks of the East, the Jesus prayer: "Lord Jesus Christ, Son of the living God, have mercy on

---

13. John 6:41
14. John 8:12
15. John 11:25
16. John 14:6
17. John 15:1 ·
18. John 18:6
19. John 14:6

me, a sinner." This Jesus prayer is very suitable for us to pray as we are about our work here in the gardens. It brings us into the presence of God and helps us to stay there in the realization that we need his mercy offered to us through Jesus. We have a variety of ways of centering ourselves on Jesus, because he is our holiness. If we abide in him, the true vine, we bear much fruit.[20] That fruit abides eternally because it is holiness. Monks seek that fruit, and so to be a monk is to trust in Jesus.

Of course, what I have to say does not apply to monks alone. You too can put your trust in Jesus and become holy. You can become like a tree with roots that reach deep down to the water. Recently more trees have been planted in the monastery grounds. You may have seen some of them as you came into the main drive. To plant a young tree is an act of hope. It is to see things from the long perspective. That is how we aim to live in the monastery: in the hope of heaven, which is eternal. Maybe those young trees are a symbol of the next generation, those to come who will believe in Jesus. They may be the young people who will come to the monastery in future years, come to pray, and maybe to stay as monks. Maybe you who read this book are one of them.

Certainly there is a good atmosphere in our woods, where we walk in groups or in pairs or on our own. The trees seem to speak good news. They talk of holiness. They talk of community. They talk of being alone with God.

You will have a chance at the end of our tour to walk through the woods beyond the other side of the monastery where most of our trees are. But there is much for us to see first, so let us carry on down the drive now.

---

20. John 15:5

Chapter Three

THE CHICKENS

Spiritual Direction

Directing our gaze to the end of the drive, we see through open gates into a graveled area. Let us go there. In it, there is a tropical-looking palm surrounded by flowers. On our right is the church, an architectural masterpiece designed by the monk Dom Paul Bellot. I shall be telling you more about it later in our visit, but first let us go in and say a prayer. The Rule of St. Benedict says that we should pray with guests when they first arrive.[1] Pause in the church for a moment to allow yourself to become aware of the atmosphere there. Some people are moved to tears by it.

Let us pray: Lord Our God, we thank you for our fellowship, and we ask you to bless this time together. As we ponder what we see, may we come to understand and accept your saving mercy and love. We ask this through Christ our Lord.

Coming out of the church, we see the porter's lodge on our right. You can leave your bag there for the time being. The Rule of St. Benedict says, "At the gate of the monastery let there be put a wise old man who knows how take a message and give a reply, and whose maturity stops him wandering off."[2] If there isn't one

---

1. Chapter 53
2. Chapter 66

14

there at the moment, there may well be one in the bookshop just along from the porter's lodge. That is more generally our point of welcome, where people who just come along can ask questions or buy books and postcards, and where telephone calls are taken. At night one of our older brothers who has a cell at the front of the monastery is available should any emergency arise. Sometimes, however, all of us are in church and there is no one at hand! I think this was the case the first time that I visited here. It was my introduction to a slower, more meditative way of life.

Coming out of the porter's lodge, you can see to the right just beyond the bookshop a couple of parlor rooms, where visitors can talk to monks, as when, for example, one wants to see a priest. For more casual chats, there are benches on areas of grass to the sides of the gravel. Going between these, through the gates and turning left, we come into the kitchen garden or *carré* (meaning square), as it used to be called by the old French monks. By this pond just inside the garden is a statue of Our Lady. Ahead of us is the tearoom, where people who visit the abbey during the day can get refreshments. On sale are little cakes made by a monk in the monastery kitchen. There is a garden area where you can wander around or drink your tea on a fine day. The peace from the abbey church seems to extend to here. People like to linger over their tea and cakes in this place.

There are pear trees along the wall by the path leading to the tea room. Like the apple trees in the main orchard, these really benefit from the shelter from the wind given by the walls round the kitchen garden area. I suppose that shelter is rather like the enclosure that we monks have in the monastery. The area of enclosure includes all our grounds, although there are not literally walls to shelter us. We are rather given shelter by our Rule, which says that we are to stay within the enclosure area unless we have to go out for a particular purpose with the permission of the abbot. Our enclosure is not as strict as that of our sisters, the nuns in Ryde, but it does give us some protection from the winds of fashion and agitation that can sweep through lives outside the monastery. It helps us to see things more in the light of eternity rather than the urgency of the moment. We believe that if we allow the light of eternity to enter our lives, it is in truth a benefit for the whole world.

If we go along this path by the pear trees and beyond the tea shop and then turn left, we shall be heading for an even stricter enclosure—that of the chickens! You will see there a wooden fence around the orchard area where their houses are, and that beyond this fence is another, electric fence. This inner fence is not to keep the chickens in but to keep the fox out. The chickens would be gobbled up very quickly if the fox could get to them. There is a sort of parallel to these defensive measures in our inner enclosure of the monastery, the cloister. On the first Sunday of Advent, which is the beginning of the liturgical year, we process round the cloister and the abbot sprinkles it with holy water. Water that has been blessed like this helps to give us protection against evil spirits. As monks we need to avoid not only the unhelpful allurements of the world but also the temptations of the evil one. Like the fox, he is cunning and seeks to trick us into things that will keep us from God.

Another means of defense against him is openness. We are told by the Rule of St. Benedict that when the cause of sin is hidden in the conscience, we should reveal it to the abbot or a senior.[3] That might mean telling it in confession or having a confidential chat with the abbot. The important thing is that we do not allow the devil to use secrecy to get us lost in a byway. For the same reason even good, spiritual things that we undertake in the special season of Lent are to be done with the abbot's permission so that we do not end up doing them for the wrong reason,

---

3. Chapter 46

feeding our own pride rather than our spiritual life.[4] We need directing if we are to escape error and self-will.

Let's go into the enclosure and see the chickens. They immediately come rushing round me because they think that I have food for them. That is stupid, because I haven't. In fact, chickens are noted for their lack of intelligence. One time the brother who was feeding them showed them the tray with the food in it, and then in front of their eyes he put it in their house. They couldn't find it and just stood there staring around blankly. But maybe we shouldn't judge them too harshly. Sometimes we are not quick to find what truly nourishes us, truly makes us happy either. I for one took a long time to come and settle here.

Jesus gave us an example of finding true nourishment when he told his disciples, "My food is to do the will of him who sent me, and to accomplish his work."[5] Only God's will for us, what he wants for us, is able to strengthen us inwardly and make us able to live in eternity. Jesus always did his Father's will, and so when we receive Jesus in holy communion we are in a sense saying that we want to be nourished by God's will. Of course, people sometimes want to be a friend of Jesus with a view to getting something less nourishing. He is the bread of life, and yet people crowded round him because when he performed a miracle of feeding, they ate their fill of the loaves.[6] They were like the chickens that crowded round us when we came in here. We are like them too when we seek some private satisfaction or special arrangements from our religion instead of simply seeking the will of God.

In the Gospels of St. Luke and St. Matthew Jesus told us how to be happy. Happiness is not to be found where we might expect it. Like the chickens, we need directions to where we are truly

---

4. Chapter 49
5. John 4:34
6. John 6:26

nourished. So Jesus tells us through St. Luke, "Blessed are you poor....Blessed are you that hunger now....Blessed are you that weep now....Blessed are you when men hate you, and when they exclude you and revile you, and cast out your name as evil, on account of the Son on Man!"[7] It's not acquiring or spending money, or stuffing our face, or finding life hugely entertaining, or being everyone's favorite person that makes us happy. Rather, it is what God, who loves us and knows what is best for us, wants for us. Through St. Matthew Jesus tells us more about this blessedness, or unsuperficial happiness. He tells us, "Blessed are the poor in spirit....Blessed are those who mourn....Blessed are the meek....Blessed are those who hunger and thirst for righteousness....Blessed are the merciful....Blessed are the pure in heart....Blessed are the peacemakers....Blessed are those who are persecuted for righteousness' sake..."[8] We are happy by knowing that we are beggars before God; by depending on him for everything; by letting God fill the empty spaces left in our hearts by the disappointments and griefs of this world; by not letting our arrogance blot out the beauty of what is set before us; by longing for what is truly good; by learning to have a compassionate heart; by wanting God above all; by being channels of peace; by sticking our necks out in the cause of justice. Directed by the words the Lord gives us in the scriptures, we monks seek the true happiness that he taught us. Of course, we have this search in common with all Christians.

We think of ourselves as searching, but the deeper reality is that the Lord is directing us to what makes for our happiness. Like the chickens, we need help to find what is good for us. Once I saw a whole clutch of chickens trying to shelter from the rain under a house here that is raised up on stilts. Of course, the rain blew in. Another chicken tried to find shelter by that bush over

---

7. Luke 6:20–22
8. Matthew 5:3–10

there. All they had to do to find proper shelter was to go up this little ladder into their waterproof house. The Catholic Church is like this chicken house. It offers shelter to all followers of the Lord Jesus. He wants us gathered together under his wing, as one of these hens here gathers her little ones together under her wing. What he said about the people of Jerusalem expresses his maternal love for all of us: "Would that even today you knew the things that make for peace!"⁹ and "How often would I have gathered your children together as a hen gathers her brood under her wings, and you would not! Behold, your house is forsaken."¹⁰ So often we are huddled shivering in the wet and the wind when our house the Church offers us the peace of the Lord.

This does not mean that the Church is perfect in all its aspects. The brother who takes care of the chickens says that the chicken house always needs cleaning. So it is with the Church: *Ecclesia semper reformanda* we say in Latin—"The Church always needs reforming." And the Church is always being renewed, thanks to the Holy Spirit who is its soul. Through the Holy Spirit, great saints arise at times of special need for the Church. An example is St. Francis of Assisi, who was inspired to bring the simplicity of the gospel back to the Church's life. Monks too have a special role. It is not as dramatic as that of St. Francis. Rather, by living the Christian life and keeping alive the Christian tradition despite the contradictory pull of the fashions of the day, monks are in a sense a point of reference. They help the mind of the Church to avoid being filled up with the rubbish of the day. You might say it is their job to keep cleaning out the chicken house. And so the Church, like this chicken house raised by stilts above the reach of the fox, continues, despite everything, to offer the peace of the Lord.

The fact that we might have really gone to seed in our lives does not make it more difficult to accept that peace. In fact, in a

---

9. Luke 19:42
10. Luke 13:34–35

way, it makes it easier. See that grass and those weeds under the trees over there? I made a discovery when I was scything that down. Grass and weeds are easier to scythe when they are long than when they are short. When we stray far from what truly nourishes, it is in a sense easier for us to turn back to good because we are more aware of our need. Like the tall grass and weeds, we are further from our roots, and so the pretensions of our false life fall more easily. The less good there is in our lives, the less real they are, because evil does not have a reality of its own: it is a misuse of what is good. So, in a way, those who are far from the true path are more liable to be invaded by the absolute reality of God than those who have settled for a comfortable mediocrity. This is what seems to be behind the words of the Apocalypse, "I know your works: you are neither cold nor hot. Would that you were cold or hot! So, because you are luke-warm, and neither cold nor hot, I will spew you out of my mouth. For you say, I am rich, I have prospered, and I need nothing; not knowing that you are wretched, pitiable, poor, blind, and naked."[11] In reality, all humankind needs the mercy of God. We do not know our spiritual condition if we think of ourselves as prospering from our own resources, or as being good because we have made ourselves good without needing what God offers us.

It follows that the desperately bad sometimes end up as the most fervent friends of God. This was my experience when I worked as a prison chaplain. People who knew only too well the darkness that was in them welcomed the light of Christ with an abandon beyond the reach of those in a bourgeois twilight. The one who is forgiven much loves much.[12] Do you see that honey-suckle bush over there? It has the most beautiful scent. Actually it is right next to where the sewerage goes. When we are rooted

11. Revelation 3:15–17
12. Luke 7:36–50

in an awareness of our own lack of sweet scentedness, God can cause his own perfumed blossoms to bloom.

While we have been talking, those chickens have wandered away completely. They haven't even left one of their number to check if we are going to produce any food for them! There was another time when the chickens showed their lack of intelligence. The brother taking care of them lined the floor of their house with newspaper instead of straw. They did not recognize it as their house and would not go in! We can be like that when we do not recognize the Church as our home because of inessentials. Maybe the style of worship changes at the place we go, or the person leading it changes. It is still our home, just as much as the chickens' house is still theirs despite having newspaper instead of straw on the floor. To refuse the spiritual shelter we are offered is to be like the chickens, led astray by inessentials.

Chicken are not the only fowl that we keep. Come back out of the orchard and past the tea shop again. Looking through the gate in the wall flanked by pear trees, we can see the geese. Let me tell you how they got into their home. Two of us stood blocking other routes for them so that we scared them into their little house. Sometimes Providence uses a method like that to get us where we need to be. Paths that we might like to go down are blocked for us, so that we end up where God wants us to be. But Providence also uses our own deepest instincts to guide us. Remarkably, a female goose will stay all day sitting on her eggs, not eating. She ignores her immediate material needs to act according to her instinct. I suppose our monastic vocation is like that. We are following our deepest instinct in being here, even if greater material success might be available elsewhere. One of the vows we take is of stability. It is as though we are saying that we want to be like that goose and do not intend to wander off and let our eggs get cold. God is surely hatching something for us!

Chapter Four

THE PIGS

Sin, Repentance, and the Advantages of Not Being a Swine

Sin is when we do not follow good instincts that lead to life, as mother goose does, but instead follow wrong desires that lead to death. If we leave this garden enclosure and turn left and then left again down the other approach to the abbey, we see creatures that can teach us all about this. Follow me and you can see them. Pigs!

It wasn't till we got these pigs that I really understood the various sayings inspired by them. If you look at this field on the right, you can see the meaning of the phrase "root around." This used to be a green field. Now it is all upturned earth because the pigs have been rooting around looking for something to eat. It reminds me of what mankind has done to the earth in its pursuit of wealth. Another phrase that makes more sense when you see pigs is the advice I received about my table manners when I was young: "Don't put your trotters in the trough!" These pigs do just this. It doesn't matter to them if they are trampling all over their food if it makes it easier for them to get it. And they have no hesitation pushing each other out of the way to reach their food. However, there is something that they don't know.

The greediest pig, the one who is most successful in getting his trotters in the trough and pushing others out of the way, soon becomes the fattest pig. And the fattest pig is the first to be shot, butchered, cooked, and eaten. As the Bible puts it, "The wages of sin is death."[1] If we allow our appetites to become so disordered that we ignore the welfare of others, our spiritual life dies. We are no longer able to be channels of God's love and so are cut off from our true life, that which endures for eternity. That does not mean that we are not part of God's plan. We do fit into his providence, but in the same sense that the greedy pig is part of the monks' plan. The pig is eaten and so contributes to the life of others. The selfish and sinful person contributes to the life of others by, for example, enabling them to develop the virtue of patience and the gift of forgiveness. Each of us belongs to God's plan one way or another: either as one who shares his life, that love which gives unity to all, or simply as meat for his providence. And we can share his life if we want to.

One way or another, God invites each person to share his life. I am very grateful to him for extending this invitation to me. As I look at the pigs here, I think of St. Paul's words to the Corinthians, "Such were some of you."[2] God in his love invited me to see beyond the pursuit of my selfish desires. If someone had suggested to me that I stop doing what I liked, that would have put me off. That was not God's way with me. He showed me something more beautiful than what I was doing. The beauty of his light drew me from the darkness in which I was living. What happened is in a way expressed by this parable of Jesus: "Again, the kingdom of heaven is like a merchant in search of fine pearls, who, on finding one pearl of great value, went and sold all that he had and bought it."[3] I say "in a way" because this parable is really about giving up good things for the sake of the kingdom, and I am speaking about giving up my bad ways for the kingdom.

---

1. Romans 6:23
2. 1 Corinthians 6:11
3. Matthew 13:45–46

However, at that time they seemed good to me, and it is a mark of the graciousness and delicacy of the way God treats us poor sinners that he allowed me to come to him as one going to something better rather than as one leaving something worse. Gentleness goes with strength, and God is all-powerful, so perhaps it is not surprising that he wins us to what makes for life by his great gentleness.

Looking at the pigs here, I think of the Lord's words, "Do not throw your pearls before swine, lest they trample them under foot and turn to attack you,"[4] and I marvel that he does not seem to have followed his own advice. The Lord came into the world that was made through him, yet the world knew him not.[5] Indeed it turned to attack him, and put him to a shameful death. And this was so that we would be able to receive that "pearl of great value" that he wants to give us. He humbles us not by his power but by his generosity so that we may come to him in love not fear,[6] as friends not slaves.[7]

Now I come to him each day in prayer. I pray the words of the psalm, "Remember not the sins of my youth or my transgressions; / according to thy steadfast love remember me, / for thy goodness' sake, O Lord!"[8] The focus is not on my sins but on the love and goodness of the Lord. One aspect of that goodness is the way he helps me to think clearly. "Good and upright is the Lord; / therefore he instructs sinners in the way."[9] In my salad days, when I was green in judgment, I imagined that everything was relative. From my selfish point of view, this was convenient as it meant that I didn't have any obligation to do anything I didn't feel

---

4. Matthew 7:6
5. John 1:10
6. 1 John 4:18
7. John 15:15
8. Psalm 25:7
9. Psalm 25:8

like doing. But it didn't make sense. It contradicted itself. If everything was relative, then it could not be absolutely true that everything was relative. What the Lord taught me was that there is something beyond myself, indeed *someone* beyond myself, who is absolute: he himself, Almighty God. This knowledge was a joyful liberation from the narrow confines of my self, which could only imprison me. Ultimately it is a liberation from death, since the autonomous self with freedom to act in the world only exists for the period we live on this earth. To tie the soul to this self is to tie it to death. To bind the soul to God is, on the contrary, to open it to unbounded life, for at death the soul goes to God who is infinite.

I don't suppose these pigs have thought all this through. Their behavior suggests that they think only of what they can get to eat. They will eat anything, except what is bitter or sour. They won't touch lemons. As monks, we try to get beyond the pig stage. The Rule of St. Benedict tells us why we sometimes have to stomach what we do not like. The Prologue observes that there may be some restrictiveness "for the sake of justice, for vices to be corrected or for the preservation of charity." The higher value of love, of getting beyond the confines of the self, justifies what the self may find bitter. This bitterness is not, however, the defining characteristic of our life. It is rather the slight pain of the initial training. The Prologue to the Rule goes on to say "In advancing in this kind of living and in faith, with the heart opened up with the unspeakable sweetness of love," there is a running in the way of God's commandments. On the physical level, the effort and pain of getting fit are superseded by the exhilaration of being able to run gladly through the countryside. On the spiritual level, that is even more true since, unlike the body, the soul does not die. The joy of its life, once found, need never be lost.

This training for eternal life is something we need to receive from others. Precisely because some things can seem bitter to the self, we cannot easily choose by ourselves what will make for true life. Even pigs when they are little do not know how to feed themselves! We could not get some piglets here to eat till we put them in a field next to some older pigs. The piglets could see what the older pigs did and do it themselves. And so they learned to eat. In the monastic life there is the tradition of asking the elders, of learning the spiritual life from those who have already been practicing it. That is part of the value of taking a vow of obedience. It helps us to learn from others what will give us life spiritually. And by being obedient to others, we get to live beyond our little selves. That opens us to the greatness of God's life.

However, this obedience is not simply subjecting ourselves to another's self. The life is lived according to the Rule, the tradition of the monastic congregation and of the house. It is not anyone's self that determines what happens. Rather, it is the spiritual wisdom that we have inherited. When we put those piglets in the field next to the big pigs, there had to be a fence between them, otherwise the big ones would have eaten the little ones! The traditional spiritual wisdom of the Rule as lived through the ages is the fence that stops our spiritual lives from being consumed by ego trips. Following this Rule together, we work to exclude egoism and to allow God to be present in our lives. All of us are doing work that has been assigned to us by others. This includes the abbot, who has a major responsibility for deciding who does what. He did not choose the work of being abbot—it was assigned to him by his monks.

Of course it is not simply the tradition mediated through others that is guiding us. For one thing we had to get to the monastery in the first place! That is the work of the Holy Spirit, who calls us here. God the Holy Spirit guides us in the monastery too, helping us, for example, to see that it is sometimes good for us to forget our own inclinations and to follow what another has determined. His work with us is rather like our work with the pigs. Pigs are very slippery animals. It is difficult to catch them to get them to be where you want them to be. They have to be lured with food. So it is with the self. It is slippery in finding reasons for getting its own way even when that is spiritually harmful. So we are lured by the delight of the Holy Spirit to this abbey, where we can give up our own selfish will and find true spiritual life. Once we are here, he gives us peace and joy in doing what makes for our spiritual life. I have felt that delight in many places in this monastery, but I will tell you more about that when we visit them. Of course there is not always delight in everything! If there were, we would still not really be getting beyond the pig stage because we would be doing things just to get the satisfaction of that delight. What God wants for us, and so what makes for our true life, is for us to love God for his own sake, not just for what he gives us.

God guides us to our true life, to himself, in many ways. The Bible says, "All things work together for good to them that love God, to them who are the called according to his purpose."[10] All things are one way or another working for our good by helping us to find God. The most fundamental of these is delight. Man, as St. Thomas Aquinas tells us, is made for happiness.[11] When the Holy Spirit gives us joy in our hearts, we are reminded of this. Times of difficulty do not contradict this. They lead us to a purer and deeper delight. There is a certain delight in lying on a couch eating bags of chips, but if this is all we do all day, refusing to involve ourselves in the difficulty of getting up off the couch, we will miss out on quite a range of delight—including fresh air and exercise!

Greater difficulties open us to greater delight. I'll say a bit more about this when we have a chance to sit down in the guesthouse, but standing here looking at the pigs who seem to embody

---

10. Romans 8:28 (King James Version)
11. *Summa Theologiae* 1a2ae1.8

a selfish lifestyle, I am reminded of St. Augustine's comment on Paul's text about all things working for good to them that love God. He was of the opinion that this even included our own sin. This is not to say that sin is a good thing, only that God is so good he draws good out of every circumstance of our life, even those circumstances into which our own wrongdoing has led us. I have found this to be true in my own life. Pig-stage experiences have involved learning that is relevant to my spiritual life.

I realize that I have been rather negative about these pigs. However, they are God's creatures so they cannot be all bad. People come to look at them and often they find the piglets lovable. What is true of the piglets is also true of our desires. Basically, they are as sweet and lovable as the piglets. It is only when they become selfish and disordered that they lead us astray. Fundamentally, it is the desire of delight, or to put it another way, love of the good and beautiful, that leads us to God. We go wrong when we settle for the less than absolutely delightful, good, and beautiful—less than God himself, in other words. In one sense we should be like this pig here basking peacefully in the sun. Our fundamental good is to put ourselves in the warmth of God's love. I don't want you to get the wrong idea about monastic life—it doesn't involve lying about all day!—but it is basically designed to open us to God who is love. We are here to drink in his warmth.

But God wants something better for us than that we should be lazy, greedy pigs. There is a parable that Jesus told which speaks of this. It is perhaps the best known of his parables, that of the prodigal son.[12] The son demanded and received the share of his father's property that fell to him, and squandered it in a far country on loose living. Instead of working on his father's estate, he led a lazy and greedy life. The result was that he ended up

---

12. Luke 15:11–32

poor and hungry, looking after pigs, "and he would gladly have fed on the pods that the swine ate."[13] Pigs don't mind how dirty their food is. The son in the parable had become like the pigs in wanting food like this, the result of behaving like a pig in the first place, caring more about pursuing his selfish desires than about his true family.

The parable teaches us how God treats us when we decide we want to get beyond the pig stage. The son decides to return from the far country to his father and says, "Father, I have sinned against heaven and before you; I am no longer worthy to be called your son; treat me as one of your hired servants."[14] He is in fact not treated as a hired servant but as a son. His father runs toward him, and embraces and kisses him. The father gives his son the best robe, a ring for his hand, and shoes for his feet. His father kills the fatted calf and says, "Let us eat and make merry."[15]

The welcome I received when I chose to move beyond the pig stage was like this. God gave me joy in my heart. This was an echo of God's own joy. When we move beyond the pig stage and turn to him, it gives joy to God and indeed all in heaven.[16] Jesus taught us this in another parable, but we'll get a better idea of that if we walk a little further down this drive and take a look at the sheep on the left.

---

13. Luke 15:16
14. Luke 15:18–19
15. Luke 15:23
16. Luke 15:7

Chapter Five

THE SHEEP

Pastoral Care in Quarr Abbey and My Earlier Experience as a Pastor

Pastoral scenes are common on the Isle of Wight. Here we have a small number of sheep and lambs. Elsewhere on the island there are large flocks. I remember seeing one when I was walking with one of the brethren on the path from Carrisbrooke toward Brighstone forest. We watched the farmer in his jeep rounding up the sheep. They followed where he led, but every so often he would ignore the ones right behind him and drive round the back of them to draw in the ones that were separated from the flock. He did this repeatedly until he had the whole flock together, following where he was leading them. Jesus spoke a parable about a scene like this:

> "What man of you, having a hundred sheep, if he has lost one of them, does not leave the ninety-nine in the wilderness, and go after the one which is lost, until he finds it? And when he has found it, he lays it on his shoulders, rejoicing. And when he comes home, he calls together his friends and his neighbors, saying to them, 'Rejoice with me, for I have found the sheep which was lost.' Just so, I tell you, there will be more joy in heaven over one

sinner who repents than over ninety-nine righteous persons who need no repentance."[1]

The delight that we experience as we draw close to God is an echo of his delight, his joy in us, which this parable expresses. We in the monastery are seeking God, but it is more true to say that God, like the shepherd in the parable, is seeking us. Getting us into the monastery is part of that process for him. It makes it easier for him to win our hearts in the monastery, as the life here is focused on him and there are fewer things to distract us from him.

Once we are in the monastery, God continues to seek us more than we seek him, even at our most fervent times. When St. Benedict writes in the Prologue to his Rule of "the heart opened up with the unspeakable sweetness of love," he is talking of love that reciprocates a love that is already there. The Benedictine life is a process of awakening to the love that God has for us. Its disciplines, such as the regular times of worship and silence, are designed to do just that. God is gentle in his love and does not shout above the noise in our lives. It is by listening to his word and being silent in his presence that we hear the strong whisper of his love.

These sheep are the opposite of the pigs we have just seen, in that they are what we want to become. Jesus says, "My sheep hear my voice."[2] By our life in the monastery, we want to be able to hear the voice of the Lord and not, like the pigs, listen only to the grunts of our own appetites. This, rather than the torpor of our faces being well stuffed, is true happiness. St. Benedict writes, "What, dearest brothers, is sweeter than this voice of the Lord inviting us?"[3] Jesus goes on to say of the ones who hear his voice,

---

1. Luke 15:3–7
2. John 10:27
3. The Rule of St. Benedict, Prologue

"I know them, and they follow me; and I give them eternal life, and they shall never perish, and no one shall snatch them out of my hand."[4] We are known personally by the Lord and by following him we find an undying life. He says to us, "I am the door of the sheep,"[5] and "if any one enters by me, he will be saved, and will go in and out and find pasture."[6] He contrasts the false seemings that the devil puts before us, to entice us into what will wreck our lives, with Jesus' purpose for us: "The thief comes only to steal and kill and destroy; I came that they may have life, and have it abundantly."[7] We have that life because "the good shepherd lays down his life for the sheep."[8] Through his sacrificial gift of himself, the Lord Jesus opens for us the fullness of life, nothing less than the life of God himself, immortal and unbounded life.

We celebrate this gift of the Good Shepherd when we sing in our monastic church the deservedly much-loved psalm, "The LORD is my shepherd." To say this is to say what follows, "I shall not want."[9] If we open our hearts to the Good Shepherd who knows his own even as he is known by them,[10] then we cannot lack anything. His grace is sufficient for us.[11] It is an infusing of the life of him through whom all things were made.[12] The sheep he has rescued proclaims, "He makes me lie down in green pastures. / He leads me beside still waters, / he restores my soul."[13] The green grass and still waters are natural symbols of peace.

---

4. John 10:27–28
5. John 10:7
6. John 10:9
7. John 10:10
8. John 10:11
9. Psalm 23:1
10. John 10:14
11. 2 Corinthians 12:9
12. John 1:3–4
13. Psalm 23:2–3

Indeed, they create what they speak of. Peace is restorative. The restoration of soul that the Good Shepherd brings is a restoration both for the human race, fallen from intimacy with God, and for the individual soul, conscious of the guilt of personal failings.

These falls, collective and personal, mean that death is inescapable, but the one whose soul the Good Shepherd restores is not afraid. He can sing, "Even though I walk through the valley of the shadow of death, / I fear no evil; / for thou art with me; / thy rod and thy staff, / they comfort me."[14] I shall tell you more about how monks view death when we visit our cemetery, but I should like for now just to comment on this phrase in the psalm, "the shadow of death." The shadow of death falls on all of us in many ways; illness and bereavement are just the most obvious. Monks, however, in a sense cultivate the shadow of death in that we aim to lead lives of detachment. I am not talking here about detachment from the world but about freedom from insistent preferences for one thing over another. It is easy, for example, for someone to become very attached to a particular work, to feel that his or her identity is tied up with it. To leave that work is a kind of death, its shadow as it were. Yet in the monastery we deliberately give up our particular work every three years, and the abbot decides if we are to do something different or go back to what we were doing. He can also move monks to different jobs during those three years. Each giving up of our position, each "shadow of death," opens us a little more to the life that we believe is eternal and so beyond death. When we sing, "thy rod and thy staff, / they comfort me," we are proclaiming our belief that God's providence is guiding us through these changes to what will give us the fullness of life. This is found in God himself, and his providence helps us not to look for it in the wrong place by getting too attached to what by itself cannot give us the

14. Psalm 23:4

fullness of life. This does not mean that we do our work half-heartedly or carelessly. Rather, we are seeking to find God by doing it as well as we can for his sake, leaving behind selfishness and self-will.

But do not think that chopping and changing are the only aspects of the monastic life! On the contrary, the idea of stability is fundamental to what we do. In fact, we take a vow of stability, promising not to give up being a monk. The spiritual discipline of giving up our own will and, for example, readily accepting moving from one job to another would not work if there were the easy option of giving up the monastic life. So when we sing, "I shall dwell in the house of the Lord for ever,"[15] we really mean it! I remember one senior monk saying, just a few weeks before his death, "Fancy spending the rest of your life in church!" This is exactly what he did, from when he was a young man till he was an old man; then, for a few weeks before his death, he was not well enough to come to church. It is precisely this sort of fidelity that opens us to God's holiness. The church here is like a slow-cooker. When we have spent a lot of time in church, we become tender-hearted like our God who is all tenderness and compassion. This is the result of being in the presence of God. When we take our vow of stability, to dwell in the house of the Lord forever, we are asserting our belief in what the psalm says: "Surely goodness and mercy shall follow me / all the days of my life."[16]

We believe in the promise the Good Shepherd makes to his sheep when he says through the prophet,

> They shall feed along the ways,
>   on all bare heights shall be their pasture;
> they shall not hunger or thirst,

---

15. Psalm 23:6
16. Psalm 23:6

> neither scorching wind nor sun shall smite them,
> for he who has pity on them will lead them,
>   and by springs of water will guide them.[17]

We are those sheep being looked after by the Good Shepherd. He feeds us with the gift of his Body and Blood and gives us to drink of his Spirit, guiding us by that same Spirit. Already, in gathering this monastic community, God has fulfilled the promise made through the prophet Ezekiel,

> I myself will search for my sheep, and will seek them out. As a shepherd seeks out his flock when some of his sheep have been scattered abroad, so will I seek out my sheep; and I will rescue them from all places where they have been scattered on a day of clouds and thick darkness. And I will bring them out from the peoples, and will gather them from the countries, and will bring them into their own land.[18]

Each of us here feel that the monastery is, in a way personal to us, our "own land." It is God himself who has brought us here by whatever combination of circumstances, influences, and inner inspiration. God has found us despite darkness of mind and soul. And he has brought us here from many different countries. Part of the joy of being here is the international character of the community, with so many different cultures and backgrounds represented. It is a Pentecostal miracle.

Not only do the sheep gathered here in the Lord's flock come from different backgrounds, they also have different needs, and so he says through the prophet, "I will seek the lost, and I will bring back the strayed, and I will bind up the crippled, and I will

---

17. Isaiah 49:9–10
18. Ezekiel 34:11–13

strengthen the weak, and the fat and the strong I will watch over; I will feed them in justice."[19] This is reflected in what our Rule says about how the abbot should look after the monks. The abbot is believed to act in place of Christ in the monastery,[20] and so he is guided by the Rule to act as the Good Shepherd, "to rule souls and serve people of many humors: one with soothing, another with reproaches, another with advice, according to the nature or intelligence of each, so that he conforms and adapts himself to all, so that not only does he not suffer any losses to the flock entrusted to him, but may rejoice in the growth of a good flock."[21] The Rule makes it clear that he is a shepherd. He is there not just to adjudicate among interests but to help those in his care to transcend self-will. The style of government of a monastery is not military, but pastoral. He is to scour the rust of sin from the soul entrusted to him, but he is not to do it so vigorously that he breaks the receptacle. He should take pains to be loved rather than to be feared.[22]

In this he is like Christ who humbled himself for the sake of his sheep. If you look at these animals here in the field, you will see that the smallest—and also the most endearing of them—are the lambs. Christ is the Lamb of God. On Good Friday we hear of how he was "like a lamb that is led to the slaughter."[23] In the liturgy for Easter Day we sing, before the reading of the Gospel, of how "the sheep are ransomed by the Lamb." The Lord Christ "emptied himself, taking the form of a servant, being born in the likeness of men. And being found in human form he humbled himself and became obedient unto death, even death on a cross."[24]

---

19. Ezekiel 34:16
20. The Rule of St. Benedict, Chapter 2
21. The Rule of St. Benedict, Chapter 2
22. The Rule of St. Benedict, Chapter 64
23. Isaiah 53:7
24. Philippians 2:7–8

Being small is the way he reaches us. Being a child, being weak, and suffering, he comes down to our level so that we may rise to his. The Lamb rescues us.

This teaches us how we should give pastoral care. It is much easier to receive a correction, or even an honest statement of our condition, from someone who is humble. Christian leadership, after the model of Christ who washed his disciples' feet, is humble and does not exalt the self. That is humility before the dignity of the other person, but it is also humility before the truth, which cannot give itself the right to overlook wrong. The abbot of the monastery carries a crosier during the celebration of important ceremonies. This symbolizes his role as a good shepherd, ready to pull back a sheep from the briars or a precipice. St. Benedict says, "Let the holy example of the Good Shepherd be imitated. Leaving the ninety-nine sheep in the mountains, he went to seek the one sheep that had wandered. He had so much compassion on its weakness that he deigned to put it on his sacred shoulders and so bring it back to the flock."[25]

This is addressed to the abbot, but it is also relevant to all the priests of the monastery who give pastoral care in one way or another. This may be pastoral care given to guests. In fact, Christ the Good Shepherd worked so efficaciously through one guest master here, that one of the guests wrote a best-selling book about him, subtitled "the man who saved my soul" (Tony Hendra, author of *Father Joe*). The abbot's deputy, the prior, and the novice master—the priest who looks after monks in formation—have a special share in the abbot's pastoral care for monks. And here at Quarr Abbey the priests also have a special responsibility for the pastoral care of our sisters in the Abbey of Saint Cecilia.

The Abbey of Saint Cecilia is along the coast to the east at Ryde, the port by which many visitors to the Isle of Wight enter.

---

25. The Rule of St. Benedict, Chapter 27, alluding to Luke 15:5

You can find it by turning left when you arrive at the pier and following the road around till you get to a Chinese restaurant, and turning left there. Each morning one of the monk priests from Quarr goes there to celebrate Mass for the sisters. In a way, this reminds me of a pastoral care that I had before I settled in this monastery. I was chaplain to a prison. Of course there were differences! For one thing, the sisters have much less contact with the outside world than the prisoners, and they do not expect to return to it. More importantly, they have different motives for being where they are. They have elected to be there, rather than being forced to be there, and while some prisoners do find God in the quiet of their cells, all the sisters are actively seeking God in their cells and indeed in their whole lives. Their sense of the beauty of God whom they seek finds expression in a particularly fine musical tradition. Their singing is of the highest standard.

But the prison work certainly corresponded to the parable of the lost sheep of which these sheep here reminded us. This was just part of the pastoral work that I undertook between the first time I came down this track to visit the abbey and finally coming down it to settle here. I also had pastoral care of a parish in the country. This taught me a lot about the generosity of God. Through the sacraments that I administered as a priest, he would give people great gifts. These they would thank me for, though I had not done anything of myself.

The goal of this priestly work is the same really as the goal of a monk's work, whether giving or receiving pastoral care. It is expressed in the prayer that Jesus makes in St. John's Gospel, where he has been praying for his disciples and he says, "I do not pray for these only, but also for those who believe in me through their word, that they may all be one; even as thou, Father, art in me, and I in thee, that they may also be in us..."[26] It is about one-

---

26. John 17:20–21

ness and so about harmony and peace: the oneness, harmony, and peace that are expressed in love for others and whose roots are in the absolute, harmony, and peace of God himself. Do you see how these sheep here are grazing together? Sheep are proverbial for their gregariousness. That is why the Lord Jesus speaks of his work, which is to bring us divine harmony and peace, as directed toward there being "one flock, one shepherd."[27] He makes a promise to us so that we should not become discouraged: "Fear not, little flock, for it is your Father's good pleasure to give you the kingdom."[28] This kingdom is the sovereignty of God: that is, oneness, harmony, and peace.

27. John 10:16
28. Luke 12:32

Chapter Six

THE BEES

Grace, and Finding It in the Context of Beauty

Grace, which builds up the kingdom, comes to us in many ways. Our celebration of Mass—the sacrament of unity—is one of the most important ways. As we wait in the cloister for the bell to ring, marking the beginning of the procession into the church for Mass, I often find myself standing right next to the rose bushes in the cloister garden. In the summer, when the winter windows have been taken down and the roses are in bloom, I can watch the bees collecting pollen from the flowers. We are like those bees in many ways. We seek grace—that is, the life of God freely given to us—and often we find it in the midst of beauty. We live in an area of outstanding natural beauty, we worship in a beautiful church, and we seek to worship with beautiful music and beautiful ceremony. Making a beeline for beauty is often a way to God. I say "often" and not "always" because I have seen a bee in the cloister garden caught in a spider's web. This reminds me of those who refrain from worship because they prefer a higher standard of beauty. The best is the enemy of the good, and sometimes we have to accept in a spirit of sacrifice what is merely good for the sake of honoring God. To be honest though, there is not all that much opportunity for making that sort of sacrifice here at the abbey. We are busy bees seeking grace in beauty, day in and day out.

Let us go and take a look at the bees that we have here. They will help me explain more to you about our way of life. If we go back down this drive and turn left alongside the pigs' field, we get to the beehives. Like the sheep, the bees live very much together, but in some ways they reflect our way of life better than the sheep do. Their society is hierarchical. So is the society of the Church. In the monastery this hierarchical organization is marked, as I said, by the abbot being believed to act in the place of Christ.[1] There is an old form of the *Exultet,* the Easter Night song of praise, which compares Christ to the mother bee. This is not just because the mother bee is the leader of the bees, it is also because bees produce wax, which is the traditional material for making candles, and the *Exultet* is sung before the paschal candle, which on Easter Night is the preeminent sign of the resurrection of Christ from the dead. So the mother bee here is, as it were, the abbot of the monastery. The bees in the hive, like the monks in the monastery, are ordered so that each has its particular role and all work together for the good of the whole. The bees are busy and so are the monks.

The bees' work is to collect pollen from the flowers so that they may have honey. Some of the monks are concerned with the care of the flowers, but more generally we are like the bees because whatever we are doing we are seeking grace. This divine sweetness can be gathered from beauty. That beauty can be the beauty of nature, the beauty of our buildings, the beauty of worship, or the beauty of a well-lived life. The motto of the Isle of Wight is "All this beauty is of God." Privileged to live in an area of outstanding natural beauty, we can receive intuitions of the divine beauty from the beauty of nature. This latter beauty inter-

---

1. Rule of St. Benedict, Chapter 2

acts with the beauty of the architecture of our church in a particularly fine way. Looking at the church from the outside, we see the deep blue of the sky harmonized beautifully with its mellow red brick. Inside the church during the day there is almost constant variety in the play of light, filtered through the leaves of trees, coming through the windows of the sanctuary. The seasons and the hours of the day give a kaleidoscopic beauty to the place that is the focus of our worship, where the tabernacle containing the Blessed Sacrament hangs.

We can be like the bees more directly by allowing ourselves to be drawn to the flowers that grow here. Their prodigal beauty speaks of God's love for us, which is there even when we are not expecting it or looking for it. The bluebells in the woods, for example, can surprise us with a sudden view of God's delicate providence, which abundantly provides natural icons of his wish to show us tenderness. The poet Wordsworth wrote, "To me the meanest flower that blows can give / Thoughts that do often lie too deep for tears."[2] This expresses well the effect of God's love. It is not just an emotional impact that is produced, that changes as the weather changes. It is deeper than that. It is the depth of peace, the peace of knowing that one is held, held in being by the Creator of all. Our calling as monks, and indeed the Christian calling, is to live in that love. That does not mean leading a life of idleness, any more than the bees being drawn to the flowers means that they are idle. We are to be like the bees, going from one flower to another. That means that we are to receive God's love so as to be able to receive more of it. This is what is called "cooperating with grace." If we say "yes" to God about one thing, that is to say, receive the blessing of his love and follow the inspiration that he puts into our heart, then we are ready for the next gift that he wants to give us. In a way, this is like a bee moving

---

2. "Ode on Intimations of Immortality from Recollections of Early Childhood," lines 204–5

from one apple blossom to another, and in the process moving the pollen that is needed for fertilization. We take what we receive from one encounter with God's love (for example, an increased confidence in him) and bring it to another encounter with his love. From this comes fruit, just as apples grow from fertilized blossoms. This fruit may take the form of the product of our work, such as some art work beautifully crafted. Or the fruit may take the form of happy relations with others. Most fundamentally, however, the fruit is in the soul.

We call this the fruit of the Spirit. St. Paul explains what it is: "The fruit of the Spirit is love, joy, peace, patience, kindness, goodness, faithfulness, gentleness, self-control."[3] These various aspects of the fruit are reflections of God's perfect beauty, which we have encountered in the different modes in which he gives us his grace.

Of course, I do not mean to imply that God gives his grace only to people who are fortunate enough to live in a beautiful place and have beautiful things happen in their lives. Indeed, when we get a chance to sit down for a more private talk, I'll tell you some of my experiences of God's grace coming through the darker side of life. However, if one is setting out to lead the spiritual life, it makes sense to settle in a beautiful place, because the beauty of nature reflects its Creator and so helps us to become aware of him. St. Paul said of God's self-manifestation through his creation, "Ever since the creation of the world his invisible nature, namely, his eternal power and deity, has been clearly perceived in the things that have been made."[4] In the grounds of our monastery we can perceive God's power in the waves that bring the tide in on our foreshore, in the winds that bring down great trees, and even in the weeds that force their way up through our paths. God's deity is reflected in the beauty of the blue sky, the

---

3. Galatians 5:22–23
4. Romans 1:20

peace of the green fields, the delightfulness of the flowers, the goodness of the fruit that we gather from our garden. All these things are passing, but they point to what never passes and give us what Wordsworth calls "unconscious intercourse with beauty / Old as creation."[5] They symbolize aspects of the divine beauty. From time immemorial the radiant sky has been a symbol of heaven—indeed, the word for them is the same in some languages. The fact that it is above us indicates our need of God's grace to reach it; indicates, in fact, our need of a Savior. Sometimes its peaceful aspect gives us a foretaste of the bliss of being completely one with God. Sometimes the clouds that darken it speak of our feeling of separation from the divine, but the rain that comes from them can have a more positive meaning. I have a memory of being in the abbey church on a winter night and experiencing the sound of the rain pouring down on the roof of the church as a great outpouring of God's mercy. The green fields are a symbol of the way in which God nurtures us with his grace. As the sheep are fed by the grass, so are we pastured by the grace given to us by the Divine Shepherd. The flowers we pass as we walk in the grounds are so many bouquets given to us by our Divine Lover. The fruit in our orchards is what we receive in our souls as the enduring result of God's grace. Since all of nature is made by God, it is not surprising that, in Wordsworth's words, "all which we behold / Is full of blessings."[6] Not least of these blessings is that God speaks to us through what he has made.

Not only does nature as we see it in today's lovely weather speak to us of our spiritual lives, its changes over the seasons also help us to understand the changes in those lives. All these plants here growing in the profusion of spring are, as it were, the first fervor of the spiritual life. It is beautiful, but it does need weeding so that what is beautiful can flourish better. Discernment is

---

5. *The Prelude,* Book 1, lines 562–63
6. "Tintern Abbey," lines 133–34

needed to know what is truly of God. That is why the monastic tradition lays such stress on the wisdom of the elders. When summer comes, it is drier. In the spiritual life the warm soft feelings that belong to a first encounter do not normally persist. God wants us to love him for himself, not to make ourselves feel good, so he weans us from the milk of these feelings and starts feeding us on the meat of his will. Faith, the deep knowledge that God loves us, replaces the more superficial feeling of his presence. We live, not to feel good, but to do his work, in the heat of the sun if necessary. Perseverance is a key monastic virtue, and if we persevere there is the beauty of the autumn. This, the time of spiritual maturity, is when the fruit of the spirit that I spoke of earlier begins to be ripe. That fruit not only nourishes others, it also contains the seeds from which other sources of that fruit will grow. A person who has reached this degree of maturity would be most likely to be elected abbot. But there is also the winter. This is the time of year when people say, "At least all this frost will kill the germs." This is the final period of purification when outwardly there seems to be nothing, but in fact God is preparing the soul to belong exclusively to him. Although physically there may be illness and death, we remember the words of the Lord: "Unless a grain of wheat falls into the earth and dies, it remains alone; but if it dies, it bears much fruit."[7]

God speaks to us through nature and its seasons, but he can also speak to us through what people have made. I have already spoken of the church here, designed by a monk. I will speak more of it when we go to visit it again, and I will tell you about the cloister when we go there. At this point in our tour, however, we can get a more general view of the buildings. Their beauty speaks of him in whose honor they were made. In a sense they articulate our search for God. Rising from the ground, they give

---

7. John 12:24

form to our efforts to reach up towards God and heaven. The arrangement of cells and other spaces enables that order that I spoke of when I compared the hierarchy of the bees with that in the monastery and the Church. It makes visible that order which allows God to be God, the only order in which we can find peace. Architecture is a skill that is extraordinarily important in shaping people's lives, and we are indeed blessed to live in a monastery largely designed by a monk.

There are other skills, too, that shape our lives toward God, by reflecting his beauty. Music is an obvious one. One evening I was praying silently in our church, hidden away in one of the side chapels off the sanctuary at the east end. I heard someone come in at the back of the church. I don't who it was, but I heard him singing. I can't even be sure of the language, but I know it was sacred song. There was something of God in that voice. When he had finished, my prayer seemed to be impoverished because that voice no longer spoke for me in the beauty of its song. It sounded as though it were from the liturgy of the Eastern Rite.

I say jokingly that we are "Eastern Wight" monks, but in fact we have a tradition that belongs to the West, that of Gregorian chant. In it, sacred texts in Latin taken from the Bible or the writings of the church fathers are sung to music that is wonderfully harmonious with their meaning. Over time the sung repetition of these texts mean that they sink deep into the soul, so that they make present the mysteries that they articulate. For example, at Christmas time, one of the key texts sung is from the beginning of St. John's Gospel, *verbum caro factum est*.[8] That means "the Word became flesh" and is St. John's description of the mystery of God becoming the Man Jesus Christ. As we sing these words, we are allowing the life of Christ himself to be present within and among us. In the beauty of the song this life is realized in some measure.

---

8. John 1:14

It is not just the singing that makes up the beauty of our worship. The whole of the liturgy is designed to reflect the beauty of God. For example, on solemn celebrations of Vespers (the evening worship), the monk presiding and all four of the monks leading the singing wear richly embroidered copes. There will be incense rising from the altar through the shafts of light coming from the windows. The coordination of the movements of the monks in worship will also aim to reflect God's beauty. It is not exactly ballet, but neither is it a random bunch of people who happen to turn up in the same place.

Dom Guéranger, the founder of the monastic tradition to which we belong, was concerned about the effect of all this on the heart. "Unction" he called it. It is a softening of the heart that opens it to God's beauty and love. The liturgy is an outward form by which the Holy Spirit can touch the heart.

Of course, we do not see each other only in church and so we are not striving only for the beauty of coordinated movement in the liturgy. We also want, however falteringly, to be beautiful in how we treat one another outside of church. Our Rule says, "Let no one follow what he judges useful for himself, but rather what is so for another."[9] In seeking this kind of beauty we are aiming to reflect the beauty of another, Our Lord Jesus Christ. Indeed, any beauty in us is only a reflection of his beauty. To speak of him our tradition uses the words of the Song of Songs, "Yea, he is altogether lovely."[10]

The loveliness of the Savior is not always apparent, however. Indeed, scripture speaks of him in his suffering as being quite the opposite.

> He had no form or comeliness that we should look at him,
>   and no beauty that we should desire him.

---

9. Chapter 72
10. Song of Solomon 5:16 (King James Version)

> He was despised and rejected by men;
> a man of sorrows, and acquainted with grief;
> and as one from whom men hide their faces
> he was despised, and we esteemed him not.[11]

Jesus is the One who shows us who God is,[12] so it follows that we do not have contact with God only when everything in the garden is lovely. God can reach us at the darker times of our lives. In fact, perhaps he has more opportunity to do so at these times because when we don't like what this world is offering us, we are less likely to be tempted to prefer it to its Maker. Times of suffering can be times of great spiritual growth. But it doesn't follow that it is good to make others suffer, so I think I should let you have a bit of a rest now!

---

11. Isaiah 53:2–3
12. John 14:9

Chapter Seven

THE GUESTHOUSE

My Experience as a Guest, and Grace in the Context of Suffering

Suffering in the heat of the day, maybe you need a break. Let me show you your room in the guesthouse. You can put your bag in it, and then we can sit down in the guests' sitting room for a coffee and a chat. We come up the staircase from the porter's lodge where you can pick up your bag and take it to the guest wing. This staircase has a very strong association for me. It is a place where, as a guest myself, I was very much aware of the presence of God. Actually, I can feel it now.

The times I have spent here as a guest have meant so much to me. To put it simply, because of them I have known that God is real, even when things have been difficult. So it warms my heart to see young guests here who are touched by the presence of God, who come back again and again, and who say things like, "The more I stay here, the more I like it."

You can see in this sitting room various spiritual books for the guests to read. It was here that I first discovered some of the most important spiritual influences in my life. From one of these shelves I first picked up *The Story of a Soul*, the autobiography of St. Thérèse of Lisieux. I knew at once that this was high-octane spiritual fuel. And over the years I have found a word for me from Thérèse about virtually every aspect of the spiritual and religious life. One thing she has explained to me particularly clearly is the way in which God can use difficult times, times of suffering, to give us his grace, to share his life with us. Out there by the bees we were talking about how God can touch us through the beauty of nature. But this is not his only way of reaching us. He can also reach us in the emptiness of our sorrow. As Jesus said, "Blessed are those who mourn, for they shall be comforted."[1]

It was actually reading here at Quarr something by St. John of the Cross (a great influence on St. Thérèse) that I first began to understand this apparent paradox, that God's blessing is there for us when we are troubled by our loss. This insight was a great grace that moved me much. Later, I was to devote a book to thinking about it.[2] Long before that, however, I came to know something of it through my own experience.

In those days I worked as a teacher. It was summer holiday time and I was about to set off to Quarr for a retreat. I was reading the newspaper over breakfast and I saw a short article that said a teenager had been murdered by gate-crashers at a party. He had the same name and lived in the same town as one of my pupils! A phone call soon established that it was he. On the way to the station I stopped at a newspaper shop. It was front-page news in several of the papers. I bought them, and with a heavy heart read them on the train down to Portsmouth. I prayed much for him during the retreat. A timely funeral was not possible as there was a murder investigation under way, but there was a requiem Mass for him on the day my stay at Quarr ended. So I left earlier than planned to attend it. As I walked down to the ferry, I could see black clouds in the sky, but there, peeping out from underneath them, was the bright and dawning sun. This, I came to understand, was an image of the way God's love and

---

1. Matthew 5:4

2. *Paradise on Earth: Exploring a Christian Response to Suffering* (Kevin Mayhew, 1993).

mercy are always there for us, even in the darkest of times. Sometimes clouds hide them from view, but if we have once seen the sun, we know that it is there. Standing by the water that early morning, I knew that God was in all of this. It did not matter if the sorrow that we felt was going to obscure the feeling that he was there; like the sun he would still be there.

On the train on the way back I read *The Imitation of Christ*. This classic spiritual book gives a very different angle on times of trouble than the one that people are generally encouraged to take. It says, "When you get to this point, that tribulation is sweet to you and you savor it for Christ, then consider it is well with you, because you have found paradise on earth."[3] I was later to take the last three words of this as the title of my book reflecting on the Christian response to suffering. At that time, I simply grieved. I returned in time to buy a black tie and then, as I joined distressed colleagues and pupils in the church, the sadness of what had happened took hold of me.

The actual funeral was some months later. At it, the priest reflected on the difficulty and grief of those months and he said, "It has been a time of great grace." Grace, God's life that he wants to share with us, had come into our hearts. "Blessed are those who mourn, for they shall be comforted."[4] These words of the gospel are true. God, who created the whole world, is infinitely greater and more wonderful than anything that this world can give us. When what we cherish in this world is taken away from us, when the transitory can no longer satisfy, we often look beyond it to the wonder of God. Trust, which was invested in what passes as a source of happiness, is given instead to God. Hope, which looked from one moment to the next for happiness, is instead invested in the eternal moment, the now of God. Love, which locked the heart onto what must decay, is transferred to

---

3. Book Two, Chapter 12, my translation
4. Matthew 5:4

the One who "is the same yesterday and today and for ever."[5] Happiness no longer depends on particular wishes about outcomes and events, but instead is found in whatever happens because this is accepted as the expressed love of One who loves us beyond words and who wants by this particular harmony played in creation to win from us the love that will make us eternally happy.

God is there when our lives are made difficult by the things that happen to us. He is also there when our lives are made difficult by the things that we do ourselves, even those things that take us away from him; that is, our sins. Our very failure to live according to his will alerts us to our need of him and motivates us to come and receive his mercy. That can be an experience of the closeness of God. I had such an experience here in one of the rooms of this guest wing. I was taking the opportunity of being here to make my confession. In this place, I had such a strong awareness of God's loving mercy toward me I felt able, and indeed eager, to be particularly open about my sins and my sinful tendencies. I was very aware of the presence of Christ as the monk absolved me from my sins.

After having checked that I wasn't feeling desperate about my spiritual state, he gave me as a penance the recitation of the *Miserere*. This psalm is an extraordinarily eloquent articulation of the way in which openness before God about one's failings leads to receiving the fullness of his merciful love. It is traditionally supposed to have been composed by David when he had sinned by putting a man in the thick of battle where he would be killed so as to take his wife for himself.[6] It is a psalm that we sing on Good Friday and also every week.

The psalm helps us to get a proper perspective on our relationship with God. This depends not on our goodness, but on

---

5. Hebrews 13:8
6. 2 Samuel 11:2–27

God's. It starts with an emphasis on his love and mercy: "Have mercy on me, O God, / according to thy steadfast love; / according to thy abundant mercy / blot out my transgressions."[7] There is no claim of one's own righteousness here, rather a claim of God's goodness. This gives a useful understanding of what confession is. It is not so much being negative about oneself (which does not really help one to be a joy for others) as being positive about God, allowing him to be God, the identifying source of what is right and good. This "letting God be God" enables one to be carefree, knowing that, in one's poverty, there is another to whom one can look for goodness, and so be a joy for others to be around. God's love and mercy are the fundamental things that we come here for. We do not expect to be instantly transformed by them. It is rather a process, like a long cycle in the washing machine, so we pray, "Wash me thoroughly from my iniquity, / and cleanse me from my sin!"[8] An essential part of this process is to know that we need it, so we sing, "I know my transgressions, / and my sin is ever before me."[9] God alone is the measure of what is right. It is not a question of whether or not we conform with the society around us. We bow before the sovereignty of God, confessing, "Against thee, thee only, have I sinned, / and done that which is evil in thy sight."[10] We acknowledge the justice of God: "Thou art justified in thy sentence / and blameless in thy judgement."[11]

Our aim is inward transformation—that the stirrings of the heart are in accord with God's will—so we pray, "Behold, thou desirest truth in the inward being; / therefore teach me wisdom in my secret heart."[12] Purity of heart is the monastic goal, according

---

7. Psalm 51:1
8. Psalm 51:2
9. Psalm 51:3
10. Psalm 51:4
11. Psalm 51:4
12. Psalm 51:6

to the desert fathers whose teaching John Cassian records. This is accomplished by God's power, which is invoked in the psalm: "Purge me with hyssop, and I shall be clean; / wash me, and I shall be whiter than snow."[13] Purity of heart is not knowing that one has never sinned; it is wanting at the present moment what God wants with all one's heart. Attached to it is the promise of seeing God.[14] With it comes the joy that the psalm asks for: "Fill me with joy and gladness; / let the bones which thou hast broken rejoice. / Hide thy face from my sins, / and blot out all my iniquities."[15]

Essentially this is the joy of the Holy Spirit. When I was absolved from my sins that day in the guesthouse, I heard the words, "God the Father of mercies, through the death and resurrection of his Son, has reconciled the world to himself and sent the Holy Spirit among us for the forgiveness of sins." These words were the fulfillment of what the Lord said to his disciples following his resurrection, "Receive the Holy Spirit. If you forgive the sins of any, they are forgiven."[16] The psalm links the purity of heart given by God with the Holy Spirit and with joy:

> Create in me a clean heart, O God,
>   and put a new and right spirit within me.
> Cast me not away from thy presence,
>   and take not thy holy Spirit from me.
> Restore to me the joy of thy salvation,
>   and uphold me with a willing spirit.[17]

This cleansing, this spiritual presence, this joy, is what enables our worship. It is a free gift of God. He does all the work,

---

13. Psalm 51:7
14. Matthew 5:8
15. Psalm 51:8–9
16. John 20:.22–23
17. Psalm 51:10–12

as it were, of preparing us for worship. So each morning, the first words we utter as we begin our worship in church are taken from this same psalm: "O Lord, open thou my lips, / and my mouth shall show forth thy praise."[18] God sets us free from sin so that we may joyfully praise him.

Of course, not all of my memories of the guesthouse are connected with suffering and sin! There are also times when God has spoken to me here quite outside of that context. One such time is through a verse in the Bible. I can honestly say that he said more to me through this verse than he has when I have read the entire Bible through from cover to cover. With the word of God it is not the quantity that counts but whether you receive it into your heart, and this verse I did so receive. It meant so much to me as I was embarking on my spiritual search. It said simply, "Seek, and you will find."[19] I was also touched to hear at Quarr for the first time the words of the fourth Eucharistic Prayer used at Mass, when we pray for "all who seek you with a sincere heart." God has answered this prayer for me. My seeking has certainly led to finding. To put it more accurately, my openness to God's seeking me has allowed him to find me. I have also found the truth of the Lord's saying about the necessities of life being given to the seeker of God's kingdom and his righteousness.[20] More than that, I know something of the truth of the Lord's promise, "There is no one who has left house or brothers or sisters or mother or father or children or lands, for my sake and for the gospel, who will not receive a hundredfold now in this time, houses and brothers and sisters and mothers and children and lands…"[21] For Christ, we leave places and people behind, but in

18. Psalm 51:15
19. Luke 11:9
20. Matthew 6:33
21. Mark 10:29–30

Christ we find places and people. There is welcome in places that belong to Christ and fellowship with others who belong to him.

We aim to offer this welcome ourselves to those who come to the monastery. It is Christ's house, and he says that to welcome a stranger is to welcome him.[22] The Rule of St. Benedict tells us that "all guests arriving are to be received as Christ."[23] It also says, however, that unless they have been assigned this particular responsibility, monks are not to speak to guests beyond giving a humble greeting when they meet.[24] From my own experience of staying as a guest here, I would say that this is not as unfriendly as it sounds. The experience is one of being loved without being pestered. More fundamentally, it is a way of being able to experience God's love. If there were talking all the time, however friendly and well meant, there would not be the silence in which God is allowed to speak to the heart. He is, as Elijah discovered, not in the wind, the earthquake, or the fire, but in the still small voice.[25] We hope to give guests the possibility of hearing that still small voice.

Of course, our part is simply not to get in the way: it is not our gift. Indeed, this monastery being experienced by many as a place where the divine presence can be easily felt may have more to do with people who were here long before us. One guest commented that there is an energy here that seems to come from beyond the particular people and the buildings present. My own intuition is that it has something to do with the Cistercian monks that were on this site up until the time of dissolution of the monasteries. The ruins of their monastery can still be seen. Let me take you there.

---

22. Matthew 25:35
23. Chapter 53
24. Chapter 53
25. 1 Kings 19:11–13

Chapter Eight

THE RUINS

The Nearby Remains of a Cistercian Monastery, and the Value of Tradition

Tradition is a felt presence on the site of the ruins of the old monastery of Quarr. Many people have remarked on the sense of the sacred associated with it. We can approach it by going down the drive along which we arrived and then turning left down the bridle way. Passing on our right a field with cows and on our left a couple of small houses, we come to a point from which we can see the ruins of the Cistercian abbey. Standing on the north side of the bridle path and looking at the ruins, we are actually on the very spot where these monks worshipped. Their church, which is no longer standing, was here. To be still and quiet here is to be able to feel the spiritual presence associated with the worship of these earlier monks. They are handing on to us what was precious to them.

Being open to tradition is receiving what has been handed on by earlier generations. In a sense it is a kind of unselfishness. We learn not to be selfish by being encouraged to see things from others' point of view. Understanding others' needs and insights helps us get beyond the false idea that our own self is the be-all and end-all of creation. Then as we grow older, we learn to take responsibility for the generation that is to come, through procreation, nurture, and education. Associated with this responsibility is the need to care for the environment, so that those who come after us can have the means of life. Both of these ways of being unselfish are fairly generally recognized, if not always adhered to. However, less generally recognized is the unselfishness of allowing a voice to those who have gone before us. All too readily we assume that the way we now think is necessarily superior to the way those who went before us thought. I call this *epochism* because it exalts one's own epoch to the contempt of other epochs.

Epochism is a kind of unwisdom. Its opposite is a sense of tradition, an openness to the values that guided the lives of those before us. Tradition is important because it enables us to receive their wisdom and their wisdom is important because it teaches us how to be open to God. It is in our relation to God that we learn to be truly unselfish. In relation to others we are always able to say, "Their point of view has no more importance than my own." Only God is God, truth itself.

This is why tradition is so important for monks. "Asking the elders" has been important since the time of the first monks in the desert, and to be a monk is still to want to learn from the fathers and mothers of the Church. It is to receive the truth of Christ as it has been passed down through generation after generation. However, there are very few places like St. Catherine's of Sinai, which I told you about earlier, where this has gone on uninterruptedly since the early years of the tradition. More usually there have been ruptures and dislocations. Nonetheless, the providence of God has used these as means of seeing that tradition is passed on. It is said of God that he writes straight with crooked lines, and this is evident in the history of Quarr Abbey.

In one sense this history began with the French Revolution. This was a huge rupture with the religious tradition of France. "Reason" was enthroned on the altar of Notre Dame Cathedral in Paris. Man, not God, was to be the measure of all. Even the traditional method of marking the passing of time was abandoned in favor of a new calendar. Many, like the Carmelite nuns who were guillotined, died because of their fidelity to spiritual tradition. But, as the Church has known since its early centuries, the blood of martyrs is the seed of Christians, and from this land watered by their blood grew anew a monastic life remarkable for its inspired fidelity to tradition. In a country where there were now no monks at all, Prosper Guéranger refounded the Benedictine order. As a young man, he read so much it made him ill, but from his extraordinary learning came a knowledge of Christian tradition that was to nourish his monks when he became the first abbot of Solesmes. The same rhythm of life and the same sacred texts that had nourished the faith of monks of old once again opened up the possibility of a deep spiritual life for those who dedicated themselves to following the way of St. Benedict.

As time went on, the extreme hostility toward the Church that characterized the French Revolution had abated, but there were still currents in French society that were not friendly to what the monks were doing. As contemplatives, they could not be fitted into utilitarian categories as being of benefit to society. Their legal position became more difficult. The abbot of the time, Paul Delatte, decided to lead his monks into exile, and the start of the twentieth century saw them settled in Appuldurcombe House, not far from Ventor in the south of the Isle of Wight. This house was leased, and when the lease expired, the monks hoped to buy it. However, the asking price was too high. This apparent setback was Providence at work. It led to the monks acquiring, at the suggestion of the bishop who used to walk that way, Quarr Abbey House. This is the stone house that you can see next to the red brick monastery. Queen Victoria used to come to it.

But it was not the fact that a royal presence had been here that drew the monks to this site. It was the fact that there had been a monastic presence here before. Indeed, the special spiritual character of Quarr Abbey does seem to come in some measure from the hallowing of the site by the worship of the monks of old Quarr. We feel a spiritual bond with them and often pray for them at Mass. Part of the unselfishness that comes from taking those who went before us seriously is prayer for those who have died. As a general practice in England, this prayer came to an end at about the same as the dissolution of the monasteries.[1] But it happens in this monastery. It may well be that the old Quarr monks pray for us. Perhaps a prayer was offered for us by one of them even before he left this world. In my imagination I see a monk of old Quarr being asked by the Lord to accept the sad fact of the dissolution of his monastery, and saying in return: "I accept your will, Lord, but I ask that one day there will again be monks in this place." Then the Lord, who is the Master of all time, used the dislocation of monastic life in Solesmes and the rupture of monastic life in England to enable our life as monks to be lived here.

This is characteristic of the way the Lord works, bringing victory out of defeat. The Christian faith was born following the total defeat of the crucifixion of Our Lord. The victory of his resurrection was the beginning of the life he came to bring us, which persecution and oppression have made only more vigorous and widespread. The year of the dissolution of the old abbey of Quarr was 1536, three hundred and four years after it began. The date was July 22, the feast of St. Mary Magdalene. Aptly, the gospel reading for her feast tells of an experience of loss turning into one of gain. In it, Mary, grief-stricken by the death of her Lord, has had that grief intensified by the seeming discovery that someone has stolen the body of the Lord. Yet turning round, she sees Jesus.[2] This speaks to us of how the loss of their home by the

---

1. This process is described in *Beliefs and the Dead in Reformation England* by Peter Marshall (Oxford: Oxford University Press, 2002).
   2. John 20:11–14

Solesmes monks and the loss of its monastery by the Isle of Wight came together and led to the finding, and founding, of new monastic life on the island. Of course, at the time, the experience would not have been recognized as a positive one by either the French or the English monks. Nor was it at first a positive experience for Mary Magdalene. She thought the person she saw was the gardener, and it was only when he called her by name that she recognized Jesus the Lord.[3]

In a sense the personal and the corporate experiences of loss are quintessential to Christian spiritual life. Jesus said, "He who loses his life for my sake will find it,"[4] and when we come to the monastery we do in a sense lose our life. The social contacts that we used to have are no longer so easy to maintain, we may be far away from our nearest and dearest, and we have to give up all our private property to enter the monastery definitively. Even if at first the experience of loss predominates and we do not recognize the presence of the Lord, if we persevere the Lord calls us by our name and the finding is infinitely greater than the losing.

Although we may receive many tokens of it beforehand, the fullness of this finding only comes after death. Our perseverance therefore requires faith. In a sense the perspective of faith is taking the long view, asking of each choice, "How is this going to reverberate in eternity?" You may ask, "How can you take the long view when your own nature, and the general values of the society in which you grew up, encourage you to focus on the immediate satisfaction of impulses and desires that are in truth evanescent?" The answer is that a view of life that understands it from an eternal (and, therefore, ultimately realistic) perspective is acquired by a long slow soaking of the soul in the wisdom of our tradition. The practice that is at the center of this soaking is *lectio divina,* a Latin phrase usually translated as "spiritual reading."

3. John 20:15–16
4. Matthew 10:39

First of all, this is reading the Bible. We believe that this is God's word and that it was inspired by the Holy Spirit. This same Spirit can speak to us as we read it and it can bring to our attention the eternal realities, which might escape our notice "for the things which are seen are temporal; but the things which are not seen are eternal."[5] This verse of scripture is written in my mother's handwriting in the front of a Bible given to her thirteen years before I was born, and so it speaks particularly to me of how the wisdom that is concerned with the eternal is passed down from one generation to the next. Following those who went before us, we ponder "the eternal years"[6] by dwelling on the texts of sacred scripture that speak of them. Our way of life is organized so that we can give a significant amount of time to this kind of reading.

As well as sacred scripture, *lectio divina* includes the writings of those who lived the Christian life before us and are particularly valued by the Church for their wisdom. Some of these writers are called "doctors of the Church." *Doctor* here has its Latin sense: it means "teacher." These people help us to be open to the light of Christ, "the true light that enlightens every man."[7]

One such person who was a special help to me when I was first being drawn to the spiritual life is St. Teresa of Avila. Her autobiography must be one of the most compelling ever written. One reading of it persuaded the twentieth-century philosopher Edith Stein to become a Christian. (Edith Stein went on to join the Discalced Carmelites, who were founded by St. Teresa, and Stein herself became a saint, Teresa Benedicta of the Cross, and a patron of Europe.) It is easy to see how this autobiography had such persuasive power. It does not tell you how to live the spiri-

---

5. 2 Corinthians 4:18 (King James Version)

6. A phrase used by Dom Guéranger (probably based on *annos aeternos* in the Latin text of Psalm 76:6) and quoted in the Solesmes Congregation Declarations, 29

7. John 1:9

tual life: it shows you how this life can transform a person. Early in the book, Teresa is anxious about whether she is on the right path. As she reaches spiritual maturity she attains "the glorious liberty of the children of God."[8] Reading her life one can feel the light flooding into her soul. Also important in my own reading, as I embarked on the spiritual life, was St. Teresa's commentary on the Lord's Prayer in her book *The Way of Perfection.* Her teaching about this prayer of prayers guides the reader to the practice of recollection, which is the remembering of God in preference to the passing things of this world. Commenting on the clause "who art in heaven," she tells us that this recollection can be recognized by its effect: "The soul seems to rise from play—for it sees that earthly things are but toys—and therefore mounts to higher things."[9] Another work of the saint, *The Interior Castle or The Mansions,* uses a different metaphor to describe recollection. Instead of rising, the recollected person goes within and finds God and eternity there. The soul is imagined as a castle with spaces that become more and more secure against the enemy as one goes further within. One who is in the center place cannot be drawn away by the devil from his or her communion with God.

There are also more particularly monastic writers that we are drawn to as monks. St. Bernard, like the monks who worshipped in this now-ruined monastery, was a Cistercian. He belongs to an earlier century than St. Teresa—the twelfth. He wrote a commentary on the Song of Songs that interprets this book of the Bible as speaking about the soul's love for God. St. Bernard's writing both articulates and inspires love for God. It is by pondering texts such as these that we can come to see our lives in an eternal perspective, in which our relationship with God is the central reality.

---

8. Romans 8:21

9. *The Way of Perfection,* translated by the Benedictines of Stanbrook and revised by F. Benedict Zimmerman, OCD (London: Thomas Baker, 1925) Chapter 28, page 161.

The tradition that nourishes us goes back long before St. Bernard. It starts, actually, in the desert. In the very early centuries of the Christian faith, there was so much persecution that simply to persevere in one's faith was likely to end in martyrdom. There was no question, therefore, of how one could give one's all for Christ. As the Christian faith became more established, however, people who wanted to give their all without any sullying by the compromises of society tended to go off to the desert to pray, away from the distractions of the city. This was the first experimental phase of monastic life. Gradually wisdom was acquired by the older monks. One man in particular is responsible for transmitting this tradition to us: John Cassian. He visited the ancient monks in the Middle East and wrote down their teaching in a form that those in western Europe could understand.

We still have that writing and it is our most basic source material for our monastic life. It passes onto us those first insights about what helps and what hinders the spiritual life. It is, however, raw wisdom. It has not undergone the testing of the centuries. So some of it is rather odd, and occasionally it is positively misguided, as when a monk is praised for ignoring the mistreatment of a son he has brought with him into the monastery because of the detachment and obedience this is thought to show. Nonetheless, the understanding of the desert fathers has a relevance that endures to this day. An example is the teaching that one needs to be very careful about those failings one tends to notice in other people. This is illustrated by the story of an older monk who is harsh toward a younger monk who is suffering temptations against chastity, and soon after the older monk gives way to such temptations himself. We all too easily project our darkness onto other people, and we need to be reminded that the real dividing line between good and evil runs through our own heart, not between us and selected others.

This early monastic life was lived under the guidance of those who were older and wiser, but it was essentially an individual enterprise. When it was brought to Europe, the aspect of it that concerns living with others was given more emphasis. The Rule of St. Benedict gave form to the common life, and indeed saw it as an important means of sanctification. This living as monks together is called the "cenobitic" life. This means, among other things, that we eat together—which reminds me that it will soon be time for lunch. We had better make our way to the church now for the short service of worship before the meal. Then I can tell you about the importance that eating together has in our lives!

Chapter Nine

THE REFECTORY

Eating Arrangements in the Monastery, and the Heavenly Banquet

Heaven is the goal of our life, but we do need food for the journey in the most literal sense of the word. Food has always been important in monastic life. The desert fathers were very concerned with food: concerned about fasting, but also about taking food to welcome their guests. St. Benedict himself, after spending two years on retreat in a cave, was urged by a priest who found him there on Easter Day, to partake of food. And now, among us, food is a frequent topic of conversation. We lead the cenobitic life, and so we have food in common. Attendance in the refectory is considered an obligation in the same way as attendance at worship. The refectory is in some sense a hallowed place. We normally keep silence there and prayers are said before meals.

We also have a short service of worship in the church before lunch. This is called Sext, because its traditional time is the sixth hour of the day. It consists of a hymn, some psalms, a short scripture reading, and a prayer. We gather together in the church seven times a day. Even though some of the offices (as we call the services of worship) are brief, they serve the important function of helping us to remember God. The day is sanctified by being punctuated with these offices. We do not allow a long stretch of time to pass without coming together to worship God.

After Sext, we walk in procession behind the abbot to the refectory. This helps us to keep, outside church as well as in it, the same attitude of remembering that we are in the presence of God. In church we serve God directly by our worship. In the refectory we serve him in our brothers. Each week two of us are assigned to wait on tables. A special prayer is said for these two in the church on Sunday morning. Our job is to get the food from the kitchen onto the tables, to make sure people have what they need, to offer them a second helping when it is available, and to take the dirty plates to where they will be washed up. It is a simple job, but it is important because it is a way in which our mutual service takes place. We also show this service to each other by passing the food down the tables. Eating together is not just about feeding, it is also about fellowship. We are companions on the road to heaven, that is (to give the literal meaning of *companions*), we share bread together.

And this companionship, this sharing of food and fellowship, is already an image of heaven. Heaven is where God is and God is love,[1] and love is caring about each other's needs, which is exactly what we aim to do in the refectory. There is a parable about hell in which someone visited hell and found people suffering there because they could eat only with long spoons, and their length prevented them from getting food to their mouths. Heaven had the same eating arrangements, but people simply fed each other.

In order that the mind as well as the body is fed, one of us reads to the others during the meal. There is a prayer in the church for him too, after Sext on Sunday, asking that he be kept free from an ignorant vainglory as he reads: we don't want the reading to become an ego trip.

---

1. 1 John 4:8

Of course, the most essential service to those in the refectory is that given by the cook. There is something special about cooking for people you love, and although one brother has overall responsibility for the catering, a number of us have the opportunity to share this privilege. And the pleasure of eating the food that we prepare for each other is (in its way) a foretaste of the joy of heaven.

Eating is in fact a way that sacred scripture uses to describe the joy of heaven. Jesus says, "Men will come from east and west, and from north and south, and sit at table in the kingdom of God."[2] This sitting at table is what we call "the eschatological banquet." It is the final realization of the joy for which we were made. The prophet Isaiah gives a picture of this celebration beyond death in these terms:

> On this mountain the LORD of hosts will make for all peoples
> > a feast of fat things, a feast of wine on the lees,
> > of fat things full of marrow, of wine on the lees well refined.
> And he will destroy on this mountain
> > the covering that is cast over all peoples,
> > the veil that is spread over all nations.
> He will swallow up death for ever,
> > and the Lord GOD will wipe away tears from all faces,
> > and the reproach of his people he will take away from all
> > the earth;
> > for the LORD has spoken.
> It will be said on that day,
> > "Lo, this is our God; we have waited for him, that he might
> > > save us.
> > This is the LORD; we have waited for him;
> > let us be glad and rejoice in his salvation."[3]

---

2. Luke 13:29
3. Isaiah 25:6–9

"This mountain" is a symbol of what is above the changes and troubles of this world. The "fat things" are the ultimate satisfaction of all our most profound longings. The "wine" is the joyful love that gladdens the heart. When we eat in our refectory, it is an anticipation of that satisfaction without end that we hope to know in heaven. When we drink wine (as we do on special feast days), it is an anticipation of the glad love that suffuses the blessed. Our eating and drinking give us life. Without them, we would be prey to death, and so they symbolize and anticipate that final victory over death of which the prophet speaks. For the time being, the life of heaven is hidden behind a veil. This veil is the sad aspect of this life, its separations and sorrows. But we believe that God will remove this veil, and we will know him in whom there is no separation face to face. He is immortal, and so when we know him like this there will be no more death. There will be unalloyed rejoicing.

It is not like that now, of course. We do feast and we do have some anticipation of that perfect joy, but it cannot be continuous. If there were feasting all the time, then food would in effect be our god, instead of being a symbol that points to the joy of being with God. It would be unhealthy both physically and spiritually. We would end up like the pigs. That is why we also have times of fasting. They are a different way of bringing God to mind. They remind us that God is unlike everything we know and that in order to be open to him we need to avoid locking our hearts onto anything less than him. The more empty we are, the more God can fill us. "Blessed are those who hunger and thirst for righteousness, for they shall be satisfied," says the Beatitude.[4] Our hunger and thirst for God will be satisfied if we do not block it out by trying to find our ultimate satisfaction in what cannot ultimately satisfy us.

---

4. Matthew 5:6

During the times of fasting, we eat less of course. We take a limited breakfast, for example, and while standing up. This reminds us that we take food for the journey: that is, to help us get to heaven. It is not an ultimate end in itself, even if it can at times speak of that end. We fast before major feasts, most notably Easter, but also Christmas and sometimes just for the day before an important feast. Of course this helps us enjoy the feast more—food is never so tasty as when you have been fasting—but it also faces the fact that this side of heaven, life is always going to be a varied tapestry. If we looked always to be replete with good food and merry with good wine, we would actually not enjoy life as much. Life here is enjoyed more truly when there is a wise balance that comes from the knowledge of its temporary character and the understanding that absolute, unalloyed, unqualified satisfaction is granted to us only in heaven. To seek that exclusively in this life is to frustrate the deepest desire of the human heart, which is made for God and his eternity.

We see the double aspect of our life—on the one hand enjoying good things as an anticipation of heaven, on the other longing in our emptiness for the absolute good of being with God—at its clearest in the Triduum, the three days that are the summit of everything we celebrate in our worship. It begins with the Mass of the Lord's Supper on Holy Thursday. In the church we celebrate Our Lord's gift of the Eucharist, and we recall by reenacting it his example of service in his washing of the feet of his disciples. Then in the refectory we remember the Lord's Supper in a different way as we eat together. This a meal of celebration—we are celebrating the gift that Our Lord makes of himself in the Eucharist—but it is a celebration in the knowledge that the trials of this world are still with us. We know that on the following day, Good Friday, we shall be remembering Our Lord's death on the cross. As we eat, we may call to mind that the supper in the upper room was not free from tension. St. Peter argued with his Lord about whether his feet should be washed,[5] Judas left the meal early to betray him,[6] and Our Lord knew what was to come.

Good Friday itself shows us this world most at enmity with the source of all good, so on this day above all we recognize the need of the world. During the afternoon liturgy in the church there are prayers for the needs of the world and the Church that are more comprehensive and extended than on any other day. Before the cross of Christ, we know our need. And in the refectory we do not cover the need of our souls by letting our bodies persuade us that to satisfy their need is all that has to be done. Staying hungry, we ask for what alone can give us what we most truly need: the mercy of our God.

Holy Saturday is a day of quiet waiting. Jesus has died for us, and it is not a time for feasting. We do not eat our fill. Then, that night, we celebrate the resurrection of Our Lord from the dead. The Mass of Easter night is the high point of the year. We do not wait till the break of day to begin our celebratory eating and drinking. This is heaven breaking into our world. This is God's kingdom made manifest. And so, as we gather for snacks and drinks after the worship in the church, we are anticipating that final joy and fellowship when we are one with God in heaven. And this little party itself, which is in the scriptorium, is an anticipation of the feasting that will take place on Easter Day. The solemnity of solemnities is marked by feasting of the highest grade. Our life on earth is not the perfect satisfaction of the eschatological banquet, but it does offer some anticipation in its good food, good wine, and good fellowship. This we enjoy on Easter Day. And for seven weeks, starting on this day, there is, according to our rules, no fasting.

During Lent there was less talking. Tea was taken in silence in the refectory and on Fridays there was no gathering for recre-

5. John 13:6–9
6. John 13:21–30

ation at all. We sought God in solitude. By contrast, Easter is the time of fellowship. The food and drink are signs of this. God is love,[7] and if a banquet is the symbol of scripture and tradition to express the happiness of our being with him, it is because such an occasion expresses the love for each other of those who gather for it. The Easter meals highlight the fellowship that each meal together expresses. This fellowship of the refectory is extended to our guests who come to eat with us. All of us are like the folk in the parable who were invited to the feast that a king gave for his son's wedding.[8]

In that parable the wedding hall is filled with all whom the servants could find in the streets "both bad and good."[9] Having led a good life is not a necessary qualification for coming to the monastery as a guest or, indeed, entering the monastic life. Our founder, Dom Guéranger, was insistent that penitent sinners were to be welcomed as monks, and the first saint that Our Lord welcomed into heaven after his passing from this life was the thief who said to him on the cross, "Jesus, remember me when you come in your kingly power."[10] However, the parable about the wedding feast also gives a warning by telling of the ejection of a man "without a wedding garment."[11] We are being counseled to get "white garments to clothe [us] and to keep the shame of [our] nakedness from being seen,"[12] to be among those who "have washed their robes and made them white in the blood of the Lamb,"[13] as the good thief did on the cross. That is to say, we need the mercy of God. It is explicitly asked for at the rite of monastic profession.

------

7. 1 John 4:8
8. Matthew 22:1–14
9. Matthew 22:10
10. Luke 23:42
11. Matthew 22:11–13
12. Revelation 3:18
13. Revelation 7:14

Through this mercy we are able to eat the food that Jesus eats, of which he spoke, saying, "My food is to do the will of him who sent me, and to accomplish his work."[14] Through this mercy we are able to drink the cup that he drinks.[15] If the will of the Father involves sacrifice, and if the cup is one that we would rather was taken from us,[16] we know through faith that this food and drink taken on earth will be a banquet indeed in heaven. To enable us to live according to this faith, we are given the gift of the Holy Spirit, which is the refreshment of which Our Lord promised, "Whoever drinks of the water that I shall give him will never thirst; the water that I shall give him will become in him a spring of water welling up to eternal life."[17] Indeed, for those who believe in him, he promises even more, saying, "He who believes in me, as the scripture has said, 'Out of his heart shall flow rivers of living water.'"[18] Christians are the temples of the Holy Spirit and so the vision that the prophet Ezekiel had of "a river that could not be passed through,"[19] flowing from the temple, applies to each believer in the Lord Jesus.

This is the inward refreshment that we receive, for ourselves and for others, but of course we also need the outward refreshment of the kind we receive in the refectory, and this has practical implications. For one thing, the washing up needs to be done after each meal! Yet this too is in a sense a gift of the Spirit, for it is a time of fellowship, of knowing that "by one Spirit we were all baptized into one body."[20] After lunch we have a time of recreation (when there is conversation) so washing up then is an

---

14. John 4:34
15. Matthew 20:22–23
16. Luke 22:42
17. John 4:14
18. John 7:38
19. Ezekiel 47:5
20. 1 Corinthians 12:13

opportunity to exchange words, perhaps to give our opinions of the book that is being read in the refectory. After supper in the evening is normally a time of silence and so the washing up is done silently then. Fully focused on the familiar task, we enjoy a kind of fellowship that is deeper for being unspoken. Without words, the Spirit of God, listening to whom is the heart of our lives, makes us one.

Each meal in the refectory ends with grace, a thanksgiving to God, whether said publicly, as at lunch, or privately as at supper or breakfast. And there is so much to thank God for: the food, obviously, but also the fellowship and above all his presence and his tender, gentle, always-affirming love, which gives us our fellowship and our reason for being here. We know this presence, this love, best of all when we are silent. The silence of the cloister is the heart of the monastery. Let us go out into the cloister now and perhaps you will see, or at least feel, what I mean.

Chapter Ten

THE CLOISTER

*Recollection, and Opening
the Heart to God*

Recollection is the special characteristic of the cloister, a place where we remember God. You will notice that it has four sides. It is possible to keep on going round the cloister without getting anywhere different. This is an echo of our aim not to be distracted from God. We want not to stray from our heart, where God dwells; the garth, or garden, within the cloister is a symbol of the heart. It is hidden from the world. Like Jesus, who said, "I do not receive glory from men,"[1] we do not look to this passing world for a sense of who we are, but rather to Our Father in heaven. The sheltered nature of the garth reflects our aim of protecting our hearts from entanglement in anything less than God, who alone can make us truly happy. This is not a matter of having an unfeeling heart, incapable of affection. The opposite is the case: we want our hearts to be feelingly sensitive to all the benefits that the Lord gives us, and to be gratefully loving in return, with a love that includes all those we encounter. In order to be alive with this unbounded love that comes from God, we need to avoid having any absolute other than God alone. When we seek not to be attached in any particular way, what we are saying to

---

1. John 5:41

God is, "You can make me happy in any way you choose. You know better than I do what will make me truly happy." If we took the contrary attitude and decided that we had, for example, to have a particular job to be happy, we would be saying to God, "I prefer one of your gifts to you. I have decided to try to find happiness in this gift." In doing so, we would be limiting God's life in our heart. A heart that will receive God's love only through a particular gift is not fully open to it.

Life in the monastery helps us to be open to God's love in many ways. Not only does it protect us from running around after this distraction or that distraction, it also helps us to avoid settling for anything less within the monastery. For example, as I said when we were looking at the sheep, every three years all the monks except the abbot give up their particular office or responsibility. It is for the abbot to decide if they are to continue in their work or not. He can do this at other times also according as he judges needful. The advantage of not having a fixed work is that we do not mistake what we do for who we are. We are monks, whose business is to be open to God's love. We are not people who have limited their happiness to something less, such as the satisfaction to be found in a particular job. Another help to being open to God's love, as I have already mentioned, is silence. Then there is spiritual reading, where we can read of that love, above all in the Bible. The regular worship in the church, which takes priority over other activities, puts us in contact with that love. Dom Guéranger, our founder, was very keen on "unction," which I suppose we may define as the felt presence of the Holy Spirit, who is love. The beauty and the music of the liturgy are designed to foster this.

So the real place of work for the monk is his heart. We want our hearts to become beautiful like this special garden within the cloister. To the objection that this is a rather self-centered pursuit, we would say that the opposite is the case; it is precisely about removing all aspects of the empire of the self. This is what makes a heart beautiful: having no self, but only God, who is love, within it. To engage in many activities in the world is not necessarily more loving. It can indeed be less loving if these activities have as their purpose bringing others under the empire of the self. The cloistered heart can do more good than it otherwise could if being cloistered is the way in which it is able to allow God to flourish in it. Because of his great respect for us, he takes possession of the human heart only by invitation. The cloister is the practical means by which that invitation can be ongoing. God's presence in the world is a gift beyond all other gifts. A heart that gives God to the world gives peace and harmony. The spiritual benefits are incalculable. They extend beyond place and time. This is not simply a question of prayers for a particular intention— this or that healing, for example—being made and heard, though that is not excluded. It is a question of the radiance of all that is good being present in our world.

That is why we must work on our hearts. They are like this garden here. Some things in our hearts are weeds which must be pulled up. One such weed is what St. Benedict calls in his Rule "murmuring." This is negativity about things, criticising and complaining in a destructive way. This can easily diminish love, as it can make other people feel negative as well. But getting rid of weeds of the heart must not be done in a way that damages the heart itself, which could thereby harbor even greater negativity. One of the ways in which we get rid of weeds in the cloister garden is by a special weed killer that affects only the plants on which it is sprayed. It has no effect on the ground and therefore on anything else growing in it. Our efforts to get rid of vices are to be like this. St. Benedict says in the Rule that when the abbot is correcting faults, he must be careful not to break the pot while removing the rust.[2] St. Benedict holds in tension the need to

---

2. Chapter 64

remove the source of evil with the need not to damage the one in whom in it is growing.

Of course, making a beautiful garden is not most of all about removing weeds. The main business is encouraging flowers to grow, such as these that you see in the garth. Our hearts become beautiful when flowers like this grow. Take this sweet smelling rose, for example. It is like the peace that we cultivate in our hearts; yet you see there are thorns around this rose. Our peace is not a matter of avoiding any irritation or trouble—that would be impossible—it is rather what flowers from our devotion to the one who said, "My peace I give to you; not as the world gives do I give to you."[3] It is a peace that comes from the Man of Heaven, a peace that is beyond this world. From the flower of this peace comes the beautiful scent of patience, patience amidst the thorns of irritation or trouble. These bright yellow flowers that you see here speak of the joy that we receive from the Lord's words to us, "These things I have spoken to you, that my joy may be in you, and that your joy may be full."[4] The sheltered nature of the garden of the heart allows such beautiful flowers to blossom.

This garden is not only sheltered, however; it is also protected spiritually. As I said when we were looking at the chickens, on the first Sunday of Advent the monks process around the cloister and the abbot sprinkles it and the house where we live with holy water. This blessed water will keep away evil spirits. During the procession we sing antiphons to Our Lady. The house is dedicated to her and is under her protection. The protected nature of the garden is what attracts birds here. Every spring ducks come here to breed. They have a homing instinct and come back to where they were born to have their own families. They come as we do, with our instinct for our monastic home. And swallows come here. One year they nested actually in the cloister

---

3. John 14:27
4. John 15:11

behind the statue of Our Lady. We see them all around the house. One morning when I was writing this book a whole flock of swallows swarmed outside my window. It seems as though they are drawn by the fact that this is the house of God, as the psalm says: "Even the sparrow finds a home, / and the swallow a nest for herself, / where she may lay her young / at thy altars, O Lord of hosts, / my King and my God."[5]

The birds that come—and there are many kinds—are like the graces that heaven gives to the heart that is guarded for the Lord and protected "from the snare of the fowler,"[6] and that receives this promise: "Because he cleaves to me in love, I will deliver him; / I will protect him, because he knows my name."[7] These birds do not come because of any work that we do in the garden. They simply come down from the blue sky. In the same way God gives graces—touches of his own life—to the soul as a purely heaven-sent gift. We may keep our hearts for God and receive his protection, but we do not earn these graces in any way. They are simply a gift.

One gift that I have received in this cloister is a sense of eternity, moments when I have been freed from the sense of before and after and am aware only of a now that extends without boundary and that transcends in importance all that comes and goes in my life and in the world. This is a foretaste of the ultimate reality when we live with God.

There is a clock in the corner of the garth above the level of the cloister, and it strikes eight times an hour. Each striking of this clock is a reminder for us that the present moment is given to us as an opportunity to open ourselves to eternity and the unbounded joy of God. It acts out the cry of the psalm, "O that today you would harken to his voice!"[8]

---

5. Psalm 84:3
6. Psalm 91:3
7. Psalm 91:14
8. Psalm 95:7

Another gift I have received here is a very powerful attraction to this cloister, a huge love for it. This, among other things, is what has brought me here. Of this cloister I can say, as the psalmist says of Jerusalem, that the Lord's servants "hold her stones dear."[9] God's love seems to come out of the bricks, the beautiful red bricks that were brought here from Belgium. The psalmist's exclamation is apt: "How lovely is thy dwelling place, / O Lord of hosts!"[10] The words that follow in this psalm (the same one that mentions the swallow) express the way a place dedicated to God both makes us long for heaven and gives us joy now: "My soul longs, yea, faints / for the courts of the LORD; / my heart and flesh sing for joy / to the living God."[11] On the one hand, we do not now have that final fulfillment of being with God; on the other we do have the joy of praising God. It is a blessed life: "Blessed are those who dwell in thy house, / ever singing thy praise!"[12]

The cloister is, literally, the place where we start our praise of God for the two most important services in the church: Mass and Vespers. We start our procession to these standing silently in the east and south sides of the cloister respectively. This standing is called by its Latin name *statio*. It is a time of stillness and quietness in order that we may have recollection, may remember that we are in the presence of God whom we are going to worship. We need this awareness of the presence of God in order to worship him properly. It helps us not to be distracted by what was going on before. It is a way of adjusting to the spiritual. As we stand there waiting for the bell to sound for the start of the procession, two aspects of our monastic life are apparent: solitude and community. Each of us is silent, on his own before God, and yet we

9. Psalm 102:14
10. Psalm 84:1
11. Psalm 84:2
12. Psalm 84:4

are with others who are doing the same thing. This is the special gift of the cenobitic life: to enable people to seek God in silence and solitude while at the same time having the supporting presence of others doing the same.

We seek to make God welcome in our hearts: this is the entire point of the cloister. "The kingdom of God is in the midst of you."[13] God is present in the love "when brothers dwell in unity."[14] It is also possible to read this gospel saying as "the kingdom of God is within you," and that points us to the fact that the love which is among us is received in the solitude of the heart. We do not say everything when we speak of God being in our hearts, since this is a symbol for a truth that far transcends it. If the cloister garden represents my heart, then at the same time it represents, simply by its physical size, a place where I can be. It can also be a symbol of the heart of God. In its double representation of the heart of each monk and the heart of God, it images that reciprocity of love to which the Lord invites us. "He who abides in me, and I in him, he it is that bears much fruit,"[15] he says, pointing to the outcome in eternity of this reciprocity. The invitation to it calls us to live in the heart of his love, the eternal love of the Holy Trinity: "As the Father has loved me, so have I loved you; abide in my love."[16] This abiding is living where the Lord Jesus lives, "in the bosom of the Father."[17]

We live here when we have the good will toward all that the Father shows when "he makes his sun rise on the evil and on the good, and sends rain on the just and on the unjust."[18] We live here when we live according to the Lord's commandment "that

---

13. Luke 17:21
14. Psalm 133:1
15. John 15:5
16. John 15:9
17. John 1:18
18. Matthew 5:45

you love one another as I have loved you."[19] This is the place of love: Jesus says, "If you keep my commandments, you will abide in my love, just as I have kept my Father's commandments and abide in his love."[20] This is the place of joy: Jesus says, "These things I have spoken to you, that my joy may be in you, and that your joy may be full."[21] This is the place of divine love and joy. This is the cloister and the life that it encloses.

Someone has to keep the cloister clean, and in view of the meaning with which it is charged, I am happy to say that as I write this, sweeping the cloister is my job. Of course, if I am given another job instead, I shall need to accept it so as not to close my heart to God's love! Sweeping the cloister, like most of the housecleaning work, is done on Saturday. It is an opportunity for recollection, for remembering God. It is a way of expressing my love for the life that I live for God and for my brothers here. Keeping the house clean shows that we take a wholesome pride in our way of life, that we believe he wants to give himself to us in love here, and that we care about each other.

This housework is only a small part of our work, however. I will tell you more about the other work that goes on here after None, one of the short services of worship that help us to remember God by punctuating our day. That is the bell ringing for it now. The Rule of St. Benedict says we should hurry to arrive first at the Work of God, although with all gravity and modesty,[22] so we should not stay talking any longer but go straight to the church.

---

19. John 15:12
20. John 15:10
21. John 15:11
22. Chapter 22

Chapter Eleven

THE WORKSHOPS

The Monastery Work and Its Spiritual Meaning and Advantages

W ork is an essential part of our lives as monks. It is part of
the spiritual life of monks since, as the Rule says, "idleness
is hostile to the soul."[1] The devil finds work for idle hands, and
we do not pray and invoke God's protection with the intention of
leaving openings for the evil one. A saint once had a vision of the
devil wandering around a religious house looking angry, and God
obliged him to tell the saint why: it was because everyone in that
house was busy.[2] Work, however, does not contradict the tradition of holy leisure, of time for God. In a sense it serves it by making possible the life that provides it. More importantly, however,
it is itself a time for God. We do not work simply in order to have
holiday time to be with God. Our work is itself an opportunity to
be with God.

When we were in the cloister I was telling you about recollection. Recollection is practiced there, and in the church, and in the
sacristy where we prepare for Mass, but it is not limited to these
special places. Our aim as monks is to remember God always and
everywhere. We aspire to follow the teaching of St. Paul, who said

---

1. Chapter 48
2. St. Faustina Kowalska

we should pray without ceasing. That does not mean being in church all the time saying or singing prayers out loud. It is rather attention to God coming from the heart. This can be fostered in various ways. One of them is to say in one's heart a simple, short prayer that can be repeated as often as the attention begins to wander from the Divine Presence. The Jesus prayer is such a prayer, and some of us use it: "Lord Jesus Christ, Son of the living God, have mercy on me, a sinner."

Work is a time when we can pray like this, or we can meditate on the things of God, or we can simply be attentive to the presence of God; all of these are helped by our spiritual reading. That is why work of the hands is so much part of the monastic tradition. It leaves the heart free for God. If we go back to the very beginning of the monastic life in the Egyptian desert, we find monks making baskets. The primary purpose of this was to enable attention to God. There is even one report of a monk who burned what he produced each year since it was not economic to take the baskets to market. We aim to be more practical than that. Our work either serves the needs of the brethren or produces objects that can be sold. But in either case we hope that the work will give us an opportunity to be open to God.

Apart from work that needs to be done at specific times, such as cooking, our work is done mostly during two set times in the day: between Mass and Sext (that was when we were looking at the trees and the animals) and between None and teatime. The office of None comes immediately after a recreation time when we talk with each other (the time when I was telling you about the cloister), and it helps us bring our minds back to God. Immediately after None the abbot leads us into cloister and there he leads us in a prayer: "God, Lord and master of the vineyard, you allot us our tasks and determine the just rewards of our labors. Help us to bear the burden of the day and accept your will in all things without complaint." This asks for God's help with our work, but it also asks for something more fundamental in the spiritual life: the grace to accept God's will without murmuring. Work is a spiritual discipline that helps us to give up self-will and so be more open to God, more available for him.

I would like to show you some of the work that goes on in our monastery. First of all, let us visit the bookbindery. We get to it by going down to the bottom of the stairs off the east cloister. We receive commissions to bind books, and that is carried out here. Bookbinding is an art. You can't just paste cloth or leather on the cover of a book and hope for the best. If you do that, when the paste dries, the covers of the book are pulled outward as the covering material contracts in drying. Then the book will not lie shut. For a book to be able to open and shut properly, this pull needs to be counteracted by a force pulling in the opposite direction. The endpapers of a book have a vital role to play here. When they are pasted down, and dry and contract in their turn, they pull the book back into position. In a sense the book has a life of its own, with these two forces at work in it, and it retains its suppleness and flexibility if this life is given play by the book being used.

This life of the book is like the Benedictine life. In the Benedictine life a proper balance in everything is fundamental. In particular it balances the pull of the spirit and the body. The spiritual aspect of our lives is like the cover of the book. It is really important, but we would not be able to sustain our life if we paid attention only to the spiritual. It would become unbalanced. So we also give importance to the bodily aspect of our lives, with serious attention given to food, sleep, and work with the hands. This is like the endpapers of a book. It pulls in the opposite direction to the spiritual aspect and keeps it from pulling our life out of shape, which stops us from functioning as we are meant to: sometimes fulfilling our ultimate purpose by being open to the things of heaven, sometimes (at least outwardly) shut to these things so that the body can receive its due needs and sustain us in this earthly life.

This balance in our lives does not mean that only perfectly balanced people can be monks. It is the way of salvation—that is, of healing—and so the life helps create balance where there was no balance before. People who are penitent about their earlier lives can live this life, as well as people who have less to repent of. There is a parallel to this in the art of bookbinding. Sometimes it happens that a mistake is made: some leather dye runs, for example, or a piece of cord left on the cover when it is being pressed leaves an impression. When you are binding a valuable book, you can't just throw it away if you make a mistake. The way to deal with it is to incorporate the mistake into the design that you create so that it is no longer a mistake but part of the pattern. The Lord does this in our lives. He uses the circumstances of our mistakes, and even our sins, to create the beautiful pattern of his providence. In the radiant and final beauty of the blessed in heaven, what was at the time a huge mistake becomes a part of the perfection of the finished picture. The Church proclaims this even about the first fall of mankind. *"O felix culpa,"* it proclaims during the Easter liturgy: "O happy fault, O necessary sin of Adam, which gained for us so great a Redeemer!" The spiritual greatness of Man comes from his Savior, and the Savior is given because of Man's fall. In the light of eternity, the whole picture is perfectly beautiful. In fact, says St. Thomas Aquinas citing St. Augustine, since God is the height of goodness, in no way would he allow any evil to be in his works unless he was sufficiently omnipotent and good and would make good even out of evil. It is an aspect of his infinite goodness that he allows evils to occur and draws good things out of them.[3] The bookbinder is the palest of reflections of the Almighty Artificer,

---

3. *Summa Theologiae* 1a.2.3

but the bookbinder does in his way show us how what is ugly in time can be beautiful in eternity.

Now let us look at another of our workshops. If we go back into the east cloister, along the north cloister, and then turn right and then left into the passage that runs behind the kitchen, we reach the tailor's shop. Here the principal work is the making of our habits. You will notice that we all dress in the same way. This is important for our spirituality. It has to do with avoiding what our tradition calls "singularity," which could be roughly explained as wanting to be different. If everyone is wearing the same, it is not possible to show off by having clothing that stands out from other people. By wearing the habit, we have already taken a little step toward avoiding pride and learning humility. It also has the practical advantage that we never have to waste any time wondering what to wear! Only when work or exercise or another practical reason requires it do we wear other clothes. For all other occasions we wear habits.

The habit is very important for the monastic life. Through the centuries many having the highest position—even kings—have chosen to take the habit, and it has been regarded as a great grace to die in the habit. This is because it is a sign of consecration. There is a special ceremony when someone is clothed in the habit for the first time. The abbot puts the habit on him with a prayer. It is a sign that he is putting off the old Adam—his sinful humanity—and putting on the new Adam: Christ through whom humanity is redeemed. Besides the habit, we wear a girdle, a sign that our loins are girded in readiness for the Lord. This is also a sign of chastity. Our commitment is exclusively to God. This does not mean less love, but more. In God we aim to love all people with a chaste love, that is to say, a disinterested love.

The putting on of monastic clothing is a time of joy. Having turned away from sinful ways, we are walking in a particular and serious way on the path of salvation, so we can say with the psalmist, "Thou hast turned for me my mourning into dancing; / thou hast loosed my sackcloth / and gird me with gladness, / that my soul may praise thee and not be silent."[4] It is a life undertaking so we can add, "O Lord my God, I will give thanks to thee forever."[5]

While it is true that everybody wears the same habit, there are subtle distinctions that the trained eye can notice. Some of the monks wear a slightly shorter scapular. The scapular is the cloth that hangs down at the back and the front, and it acts as a kind of work apron. The monks who do not have the full-length scapular are novices. They are still learning the basics of monastic life, and they are free to leave at any time if they decide that this is not the life for them. They can also be sent away if the abbot decides that this is not the life for them. The full-length scapular is given at first profession. This is the commitment by the monk to serve the Lord in the monastery, promising stability, conversion of life, and obedience. The first profession is a commitment for three years. A monk can leave when this expires if he decides that, after all, this life is not for him. However, the expectation is that the fundamental decision is made before first profession and that this is normally confirmed at solemn profession.

Solemn profession is made at the expiration of the first profession and it is for life. By making a life commitment to follow the Lord in the monastic way, we seek to set ourselves free from the narrowness of self-will. Although there are obvious differences, it is in some ways like making marriage promises. Once someone has promised fidelity to a spouse, a really selfish life is off-limits. In the same way we hope that our monastic commitment will help us to transcend our selfish inclinations and lead us to holiness. Like the simple profession, the solemn profession is marked by clothing. At the ceremony for it, the cowl is given.

---

4. Psalm 30:11–12
5. Psalm 30:12

This is a prayer garment that is worn only for the more solemn times of prayer in the church. It goes over the top of the habit and, since it covers us entirely, can be seen as a sign of total dedication to God.

There is one other variation in the detail of clothing. The abbot wears a cross around his neck. This is a sign of his representing Jesus, the crucified one. It also speaks of the burden of his office. Whereas other monks are accountable only for their particular field of responsibility, the abbot is accountable for everything that goes on in the monastery all the time. Any discontent felt in (or about) the monastery can end up being directed to him, even if there is nothing that he can do about it. Like Jesus, he has a cross to carry. However, normally it is not as severe as that born by our original founder, St. Benedict. His monks tried to poison him because they found him too strict!

Also in this tailor's shop, garments are made for us to wear in the church. One example is the white alb, which symbolises the purity of one who has been baptized and is worn by monks who are carrying the thurible, a covered bowl on a long chain in which the incense is burned. The alb is also worn for the celebration of Mass by monk-priests under their chasubles, which are also made here and which are a sign of priestly office and are used only for Mass. Chasubles are different colors according to the season: for example, white for Christmas and Easter, purple for Advent and Lent.

We've got time to see one more workshop before tea. Let's go to the pottery. We turn right out of the tailor's shop, go further along the corridor, then turn left and go through the locker room to the works yard. The pottery is just the other side of it. The pots that are made here are sold in our bookshop and also through exhibitions. Work can be commissioned, too. Pottery is part of the creative work that goes on here. There is also a sculptor (not a monk) who spends some time here. He has a workshop the other side of the yard. Then there is painting. Many a picture by a monk has been sold in our shop. There are also facilities for woodwork, in the tradition of St. Joseph and his Foster Child.

All this creative work is a reflection of the work of the Creator. As monks, we try to remember that however much we make and however beautiful it is, we are not ourselves the ultimate artificers. We are in fact the art work of One greater than us. We read this in the prophet Jeremiah. He is told by the Lord, "Arise, and go down to the potter's house, and there I will let you hear my words."[6] He reports what happens: "I went down to the potter's house, and there he was working at his wheel. And the vessel he was making of clay was spoiled in the potter's hand, and he reworked it into another vessel, as it seemed good to the potter to do."[7] Then Jeremiah tells us what the Lord said to him: "Can I not do with you as this potter has done?"[8] We are fashioned out of clay, as Adam was, and we do not have independent control of our destiny. Our destiny is ultimately in the hands of the Lord. What matters is our relationship with him. That needs to be our concern: our eternal happiness depends on it. Even murderous enemies can attack only our physical life, and then as unwitting agents of his providence. We are told in the gospel to be more afraid of separating ourselves from him than of those who can kill us.[9] This is more than enough reason for us to be living lives of prayer at a time when there are new and unpredictable dangers in the world.

We forget the primacy of our relationship with God through pride, when we think that we have some ultimate control. Being skilled at something opens us to this temptation: the artificer can forget the Artificer. St. Benedict is aware of this and in his Rule he

---

6. Jeremiah 18:2
7. Jeremiah 18:3–4
8. Jeremiah 18:6
9. Matthew 10:28

ordains that skills can only be practiced with the abbot's permission. If someone becomes proud because of his skill and he thinks he is doing his monastery a favor, he is to be stopped from practicing his art, unless, having seen his humility, the abbot asks him to start again.[10] The production of quality goods is also a temptation to profiteering, and so for the avoidance of avarice, the Rule of St. Benedict says that they should be sold at a little less than the going rate.[11] Monastery shops are good places to find bargains!

As we work to produce goods, whether pots or books, we may seem to be the ones doing the shaping, but actually God is shaping us. In one sense he is doing this through the abbot, who is the one who has the ultimate say about who does what, but God also does it through every member of the community. We have an influence on each other. You could say that we are being sculpted and those around us knock the rough edges off us, but our life together adds up to more than that. We give to each other in many different ways.

---

10. Rule of St. Benedict, Chapter 57
11. Chapter 57

Chapter Twelve

THE TEAROOM

Community Life and Its Spiritual Aspect

Community life is in a sense the defining characteristic of Benedictine life. The first monks were solitaries in the desert. Under the Rule of St. Benedict, monks find God both by their solitary prayer and by their life in community. We give our hearts to God in the solitude of our devotions and we show the sincerity of that gift by giving to our brothers when they need something from us. Although we spend quite a lot of time on our own, we come together at different times during the day and in several places. There is the scriptorium where we go after lunch, at least if the weather is not good. In monastic tradition the scriptorium is the place where writing is done, but actually nowadays we write in the library or in our cells, mostly on computers. In fact, our scriptorium houses a small library of books of literary or recreational interest. We go there for our celebrations after the great Masses of Christmas and Easter, as well as for coffee after lunch. Next door to the scriptorium is the tearoom. Monks are gathering for tea there now. Let us go and join them. We do not normally have guests join us for tea, but we can make an exception for you. We can get there by going back along the corridor beyond where the tailor's shop is.

Teatime is one of our recreation times when we relax together. Recreation is not our only time together as a community. Our worship in church brings us together and so does some of our work, and we meet to discuss things that need serious attention. But recreation is when we can be together without being serious. It is a time for laughing, a time for encouraging each other; it is a time when our simple humanity and its need for other people can be acknowledged. The tearoom is a good place for this. Whether by accident or design, there are only just enough chairs for us to sit on. This means that you have to sit next to someone! We don't keep a distance from each other.

There is one kind of work that we occasionally do together here, not at this time but during the recreation period immediately after lunch. That is peeling fruit or vegetables for use in the kitchen. This is in a way an extension of the fellowship of the table that I spoke of earlier in connection with the refectory. It brings us all together and is a chance to talk and joke with each other. It also gives the cooks the opportunity to produce some tasty desserts, or sauce to go with our homegrown pork.

More commonly, however, the tearoom is a place where we can simply be together. It really comes into its own in the cold weather when we have a fire lit here, fueled by logs that we have chopped ourselves from the fallen trees in our grounds. It is our fire, and it brings us together. Characteristically, we sit in a circle around the fire. To contemplate the fire is to be reminded of what, at the deepest level, brings us together. Our Lord Jesus said, "I came to cast fire upon the earth; and would that it were already kindled! I have a baptism to be baptized with; and how I am constrained until it is accomplished!"[1] He was speaking of his gift of himself on the cross, through which he has sent the Holy Spirit among us.[2] When the Holy Spirit was received by the first Christians, "there appeared to them tongues as of fire, distributed and resting on each one of them."[3] We

---

1. Luke 12:49–50
2. John 19:30
3. Acts 2:3

continue to pray for that same Spirit to be among us as fire, saying, "Come, O Holy Spirit, fill the hearts of your faithful, and enkindle in them the fire of your love." We ask this Spirit to warm what is cold in us that we may be warmhearted and there may be warmth among us. The fire that burns in this grate is a visible sign of this warmth.

It is the Holy Spirit that brings us together, not anything else. We are not gathered here together because we are of one nationality—far from it: indeed there are ten separate nations represented in this community. Yet, like those gathered together in Jerusalem on the first day of Pentecost, we all together hear the telling of "the mighty works of God," above all, that is, the mighty work of our redemption. And the Spirit makes us one body. In the words of St. Paul, "Just as the body is one and has many members, and all the members of the body, though many, are one body, so it is with Christ. For by one Spirit we were all baptized into one body."[4] Although we have different aptitudes and different skills, we are animated by the same Spirit in the service of the same Lord: "There are varieties of gifts, but the same Spirit; and there are varieties of service, but the same Lord; and there are varieties of working but it is the same God who inspires them all in every one."[5] On the practical level we serve the Lord and each other by different skills: for example, one brother is skilled in plumbing, another has qualifications in dealing with electrical wiring, and a third understands the intricacies of information technology. But on the spiritual level there are a variety of gifts too. For example, one has a gift of intuitive understanding of others, another is a channel of healing, and a third is able to pray at a deep level.

Both practically and spiritually, we aim to live like the first followers of the Lord, of whom we are told, "All who believed

---

4. 1 Corinthians 12:12–13

5. 1 Corinthians 12:4–6

were together and had all things in common; and they sold their possessions and goods and distributed them to all, as any had need."[6] We acknowledge our need of each other as members of the Body of Christ, for "the eye cannot say to the hand, 'I have no need of you,' nor again the head to the feet, 'I have no need of you.'"[7] And we share our joys and sorrows: "If one member suffers, all suffer together; if one member is honored, all rejoice together."[8]

This solidarity, though it binds together especially the monks who live here, is not limited to them. Our oblates, who try to live by the spirit of the Rule of St. Benedict although they do not reside in a monastery, have a spiritual association with us and gather together here from time to time. Our guests share in the spirit of the place too, even if they have direct contact only with a few monks. We belong to the entire Church, which we aim to serve, not least by giving priests and seminarians space and time in which to be open to the Spirit. Quarr Abbey is a place where people can find their calling in the Church, whatever it may be. And our solidarity goes beyond those who share our beliefs. It is with all humanity. In our prayers and the ordinariness of our life, we bring before God all people, wherever they may be. And it is our hope that the flame of the Spirit that burns here may be kindled also in the hearts of all these others. Although we do not have a mission in the sense of going out and running what goes on in the world, we have a spiritual mission: to be love in the heart of the Church, to burn with the flame of the Spirit that others may catch fire with that flame.

Charity begins at home, they say. This means not that we should spend all our money on ourselves but that if we are to be channels of God's love to others, it must first of all be among our-

---

6. Acts 2:44–45
7. 1 Corinthians 12:21
8. 1 Corinthians 12:26

selves. It is not an abstraction. "He who does not love his brother whom he has seen, cannot love God whom he has not seen."[9] But that love does not come from us: it comes from God. "We love, because he first loved us."[10] In our life and our liturgy, we help each other to celebrate that love.

Do you see through the window the terrace outside there? In that pond on the terrace is an image of this love that comes from God: the fountain. By leaving the network of selfish contrivances that the Bible calls "the world" and coming to the monastery, we aim to undo the state of affairs described by Jeremiah the prophet: "My people have committed two evils: they have forsaken me, the fountain of living waters, and hewed out cisterns for themselves, broken cisterns, that can hold no water."[11] We respond to the prophetic call: "Every one who thirsts, come to the waters."[12] We hear the cry of Jesus who "stood up and proclaimed, 'If any one thirst, let him come to me and drink.'"[13] In doing this we can become ourselves a source of love for others, for he also said (as I mentioned when we were talking about the refectory), "He who believes in me, as the scripture has said, 'Out of his heart shall flow rivers of living water.'"[14]

That fountain is literally as well as symbolically a center of our sharing of love, for out there on the terrace is where we gather on some of the warmer evenings of summer for a barbecue. This occasional relaxation from the normal silence of our meals is a celebration of the love that is hidden in that silence. In the silence, in the solitude, we find God who is love, and in the gathering we bring that love to others. Although we aim to be

---

9. 1 John 4:20
10. 1 John 4:19
11. Jeremiah 2:13
12. Isaiah 55:1
13. John 7:37
14. John 7:38

fountainheads of love, of course, like everybody else, we have good days and not so good days, but when we are not so bubbly there are others who have, as it were, spare capacity to help us along. That is the beauty of community: when we are down there are others to help us up, and we too can help others up when they are down. We can hardly say which is the more important: to be the one who brings love out of others, or to be the one out of whom love comes. But whether we are the Body of Christ suffering or the Body of Christ ministering, we are one Body.

Very important in this Body are those who are sick or infirm. St. Paul proclaimed, "When I am weak, then I am strong"[15] because the Lord had said to him, "My power is made perfect in weakness."[16] Human weakness impedes human egoism and self-will and so allows God's strength to be made manifest. For this reason, the weak and ill are bringers of special grace to us. The infirmary is a holy place. It is directly above the tearoom where we are and the scriptorium next door. Monks go there if they are sick enough to need special arrangements or too weak with age to cope with life in ordinary cells in the monastery. It is necessarily the place where many monks die. This gives it a special importance, for those who are about to die have already something of their destination about them. All of our life is directed towards heaven, but when that life is almost over, the radiance of its goal not uncommonly suffuses it.

Another reason why the sick are important is that in serving them we serve Our Lord Jesus Christ who explicitly identified himself with them in the parable about the last judgement: "I was sick and you visited me"[17] and "As you did it to one of the least of these my brethren, you did it to me."[18] I haven't known it here,

---

15. 2 Corinthians 12:10
16. 2 Corinthians 12:9
17. Matthew 25:36
18. Matthew 25:40

but the Rule of St. Benedict anticipates the possibility of the sick being overdemanding and says that with such as these a fuller reward is gained.[19] Whatever they are like, we gain grace from our association with the sick.

We also gain grace from our association in times of health. For example, one form our recreation takes after lunch is walking in the woods down by the sea. This is an opportunity to share thoughts either in groups or in pairs, and our faith can be built up by knowing the convictions of our brothers. We also have the chance of going out for a walk or a bicycle ride once a week, on Thursdays (except during Lent). The Isle of Wight is a very beautiful place, and God can speak to us through this beauty as well as through the fellowship of our brothers. The change of scene, fresh air, and exercise help us to be more faithful to our daily life in the monastery. There is a tradition that when we get back from an outing like this we go first of all to the church. Here we can say thank-you to God for our enjoyment, and perhaps too for the privilege of living in such a wonderful place as this abbey.

You can see that we have lots of opportunities for being with our brother monks. We aim above all to be one, as God is one. In a happy community, the prayer of Jesus, that his followers may be one even as he and the Father are One, finds in an important sense its fulfillment.[20] In the monastic tradition, one psalm in particular celebrates this unity. It begins, "Behold, how good and pleasant it is / when brothers dwell in unity!"[21] It makes two comparisons. The first is with the anointing of the priest Aaron. This unity, it says, "is like the precious oil upon the head, / running down upon the beard, / upon the beard of Aaron, / running down on the collar of his robes!"[22] This points to the sacred and super-

---

19. Chapter 36
20. John 17:11
21. Psalm 133:1
22. Psalm 133:2

natural character of our fellowship. It is also a natural gift as the psalmist suggests by comparing it to "the dew… / which falls on the mountains of Zion!"[23] You can't deserve dew: God simply and quietly gives it to you, probably while you are asleep. So it is with our fellowship. I have done nothing to deserve the fellowship of the monks who live with me. It is a quiet and simple gift of God. And in this fellowship is blessing and life, as the final words of the psalm make clear: "There the Lord has commanded the blessing, / life for evermore."[24] When a man asks formally to be a monk here, what he asks us for is "the mercy of God and fellowship with you." The two are intimately connected: in receiving mercy from God we have joy to share with our brothers, and in compassionate love for each other we open ourselves to God's compassion and love.

When we are one, in the sense celebrated by the psalm, the oneness of God is among us. If it is true that the whole is more than the sum of its parts, it is even more true that the monastery is more than the accumulation of individual persons living in it. On our own we might well struggle to keep a remembrance of God. Together, even if we wanted to, we can hardly be unaware of God's presence among us. A monastery where the monks are united is an invitation to Almighty God, who is love, to dwell on earth. That is why a properly functioning monastery is always a blessing for the world, even if this blessing has no external form in the way of services visibly rendered.

There is the bell for Vespers. It often takes us by surprise when we are chatting at tea. Go to the church now and I will see you a little while after Vespers. You can wait in the church for me. Immediately after Vespers we will be in the chapter house for our daily meeting. There we hear about the saints who are to be

---

23. Psalm 133:3
24. Psalm 133:3

remembered tomorrow, have a short reading from the Rule and a spiritual talk from the abbot. It is also an opportunity to share news with each other and to pass on any requests for prayer that we have received. At teatime we come together informally; in the chapter house, we come together formally.

Chapter Thirteen

THE LIBRARY

Vespers, and Seeking God by Reading and Studying

Seeking God is the purpose of our life in the monastery. It takes many forms. Praise of God is one of them. Reading and studying is another. In a moment I will take you to the library so that you can see what books we have, and I can tell you how we use them, but first let me tell you a bit about Vespers, which you have just attended with us. The other offices that you attended around the middle of the day were what we call "little hours"—they are rather short acts of worship—so this is the first major office that you have attended. It is important in marking the evening hour by praise of God. Coming after the tea that rounds off our afternoon work period, Vespers is a significant dividing point in our day. If we are out, as we often are on a Thursday afternoon, we consider it very important to get back for Vespers.

It begins, like all the other offices, by invoking God's help. By this help we remember him and are able to praise him. The hymn for Vespers, which comes next, sometimes makes allusion to the fading of the light, and asks for God's light to come into our hearts. Although it depends on the time of the year as to whether the daylight is actually fading at this point, it is normally a moment of transition to a more reflective time. We let the business of the day fade so as to open ourselves to spiritual light. In doing this we are in a sense anticipating the time when the business of our lives will fade and, through the gates of death, we will enter the eternal light. Our lives are a preparation for entering eternal light and each evening is as it were a rehearsal for that entry which we mark by our prayer together.

The main part of Vespers is the singing of the psalms. I'll tell you more about the singing when we visit the music room after supper, but you will have noticed that a phrase is sung before and after each psalm. This is an antiphon that gives color or a theme to the psalm. It may be special for a feast day or a particular season, like Christmas, or it may simply highlight one verse from the psalm. I have been quoting the psalms to you as we have been going around the abbey, though for Vespers (as for Compline, the last service of the day) they are in Latin. After the psalms there is a short reading from scripture and a few moments to reflect upon it. Then we sing a responsory. These are a few short phrases, normally of scriptural origin, which form a kind of melodic prayer with an element of repetition. One of them says (when translated into English): "Cleanse my soul, because I have sinned against you. I said, Lord, have mercy on me. Glory be to the Father and to the Son and to Holy Spirit..." This sums up the orientation of soul that we want to acquire: knowing that we need God's mercy, and, confident of that mercy, giving him praise. To sing words like these each day allows this attitude to gradually enter the soul.

After the responsory is the high point of Vespers, the singing of the Magnificat. This is the song of praise that Mary sang in response to the greeting of her cousin Elizabeth, as given to us in the Gospel of St. Luke.[1] Elizabeth said, "Blessed is the fruit of your womb,"[2] and Mary responded by celebrating the "great things" that God had done for her. We join our celebration to hers, for these "great things" include our redemption through

---

1. Luke 1:46–55
2. Luke 1:42

Jesus Christ. On feast days we incense the altar during the Magnificat in sign of thanksgiving to God for what he has done. In singing Mary's words we seek to conform our souls to hers, for she is uniquely humble and open to God. "Let it be to me according to your word,"[3] she said. We want to be like that because, as the Magnificat says, God scatters the proud in the imagination of their hearts and exalts those of low degree. When we look not to ourselves but to God for all that is good, he gives us himself in whom is contained all that is good. The daily recitation of the Magnificat helps us to become open to him and so to goodness.

We end Vespers with a prayer and with singing our thanks to God. Gratitude to God is the essence of a healthy spiritual life. One great spiritual teacher said it is enough to be grateful. This makes sense when we reflect that true gratitude includes doing what we can to show it. So this ending on a note of gratitude helps us to grow spiritually. After this, at the very end, we ask for God's help once more, not just for ourselves but also for those of our brothers who are absent. We pray too for the peace of those who have left this life.

You can see that we seek God in a very direct way in our worship by explicitly putting ourselves in an honest and healthy relation to him, but we also seek him by developing our understanding of the things of God. For that we have recourse to books. Let us go to the library now. It is at the end of the cloister that leads out of the church. We can go straight from where God gives us the grace of the sense of his presence to the place where we can seek to understand what is going on, by drawing on the reflections of believers through the ages.

As we come into the library, we see in front of us the books about scripture. You remember that when I invited you to spend this time with me, I said I would be drawing on two books to

---

3. Luke 1:38

explain our life here, the books of nature and of the Bible. We draw on the same resources when we seek to understand what God is doing in our lives. We need both. It is not enough for us just to look at the pigs and think, "There, but for the grace of God, go I," we also need God's word so as to allow him to speak directly to us.

I told you a little about how we do this when we were looking at the ruins. That spiritual reading is at the very heart of our lives, but it is not the only kind of reading relating to the Bible that we do. To understand well what is written in the Bible, we also need to study what scholars have written to elucidate the force that the words of the original authors had in the context in which they wrote. This gives us our starting point for going deeper into the meaning of the Bible. St. Bernard of Clairvaux said that reading the Bible like this—gathering its straightforward historical meaning—is like being in the garden gathering apples. But that can lead on to other ways of reading the Bible, also denoted by places. Ultimately, there is the mystery of divine contemplation which St. Bernard says is like the marriage bedroom. Through our pondering of scriptural texts we come to the consummation of our relationship of love with God.

This is an affair of the heart, but the mind is not excluded. It is important that we think clearly. You see on our left the philosophy books. The study of philosophy is a requirement for anyone who is to become a priest, so any monk who is to be ordained will use some of these books. They are there too for anyone who wishes to clarify and deepen their thinking. You do not need to be a deep thinker to be a monk, but deep thought is certainly not excluded from the monastic life.

Behind us, just to the right of the door, are the theology books. The study of theology is an essential part of the life of a monk. Our lives are dedicated to the contemplation of God. Of course, God transcends all that human thought can grasp, but nonetheless it helps us to be able to think what can be thought about God. These books assist us. They contain the thinking about the revelation of God made to us in Jesus Christ that has come down to us over the centuries. Foremost among the authors is St. Thomas Aquinas. His systemization and summary of the theology of the first twelve Christian centuries remains an invaluable guide to us. His writing grew out of his prayer and so our prayer can grow out of his writing. For many a monk he has been a guide to the pondering of the mysteries of God.

If we turn round and go further into the library now, penetrating beyond the scripture, we will find on the right-hand side the patristic authors and on the left the liturgical books. This is apt because both patristic writing and liturgy have as their foundation the scriptures. I have already spoken to you about the value of the writings of those who went before us in faith, when we were reflecting on tradition as we looked at the ruins. In the patristic section of the library, the earlier of those writings are collected. St. Bernard of Clairvaux is regarded as the last of the fathers of the Church, that is, the last patristic author. St. Augustine, who lived in the fourth and fifth centuries, is perhaps the most important patristic author. He has had a huge influence on the development of Christian theology. He is much quoted by St. Thomas Aquinas, for example, and his writings are often read during our first service of worship in the day, Vigils. Perhaps more special to us as monks, however, is St. Gregory the Great, who became pope in 690. He wrote the life of our founding father, St. Benedict, and included many interesting and instructive stories. For example, he tells us of a vision that St. Benedict had of creation being a very small thing in the light of God, and Gregory comments that the whole of creation is narrow to the soul seeing the Creator.[4] It may seem to one who looks on our

4. *Dialogues*, Book Two, Chapter 35

lives as monks from the outside that they are somewhat narrow, being lived mostly in one place and being concerned with the same daily routine. However, the truth is, as St. Gregory teaches us, that it is the whole wide world beyond the monastery that is narrow while God, whom we contemplate in the monastery, is unbounded. The eternal perspective is necessarily wider than the temporal perspective.

If we go now to the liturgy section of the library, I will be in the right place to give you more of an idea of how we cultivate an eternal perspective. I have already told you about the part that spiritual reading, especially of the Bible, plays in this. The books here are concerned with what we do in church, giving us texts and prayers that can be read or sung as part of our worship there. This is very important for our faith. There is a traditional saying that makes an identification between the law of praying and the law of believing: that is, what we receive from those who went before us in the way of prayers is also the faith that they pass on to us, and how we enter more deeply into that faith is by praying these prayers. Faith is our means of uniting ourselves to God, and so our use of these prayers binds us to God.

The importance of the liturgy is the central insight of the founder of our congregation and monastic mother house, Dom Guéranger. His extraordinary learning in the Christian tradition was above all learning about the liturgy. His thorough knowledge of the prayers of Christians in public worship through the ages enabled him to bring new and authentic life to the worship of his own time. Above all, through the inspiration of the Holy Spirit, he was able to restore faithfully the worship of monks. He has given us a living tradition that has been passed on from one generation of monks to the next, but he has also given us his books, although he considered his writing less important than the direction of souls. A central work is *The Liturgical Year,* which he wrote to explain the significance of the various liturgical seasons and feasts that are celebrated in the Church.

Basically, these bring before us the mystery of Christ. Each aspect of the life of Christ tells us something about God. Because Christ is God, each act of Christ shares in the divine act of being, the absolute "I am Who I am"[5] of God, and is therefore an eternal act and a window onto eternity for us. As we contemplate these different aspects in the liturgical year, we see, albeit "through a glass, darkly,"[6] a vision of eternity. To celebrate the liturgy is to begin to leave behind the narrowness of a temporal perspective and, while yet living in time, to acquire an eternal perspective. The very fact of the repetition of the same pattern of the liturgy year after year indicates that we are not making a journey in time but rather journeying beyond time, into eternity.

Jesus is the Way through whom we make this journey into eternity. The liturgical year begins with Advent, the season of looking forward to his coming, both his coming into the world as the Son of Mary and his coming at the end of time as Judge of the World. This leads to Christmas time, a season especially dear to Dom Guéranger. For him, as for us, monastic life celebrates God incarnate among us. We know that through Jesus we can lead a fully human life that will take us to God. After a period of what we call "ordinary time," the next great season is that of Lent, a time of fasting and spiritual preparation for Easter. St. Benedict says that all of a monk's life should be a Lent, but since it does not work out like this in practice monks should make a point of extra prayer and giving something up for this season.[7] I told you something about this season and about the Easter celebrations when we were speaking of food in connection with the refectory. These dining arrangements are a reflection of what happens in

---

5. Exodus 3:14
6. 1 Corinthians 13:12 (King James Version)
7. Chapter 49

the liturgy, and they help us live more fully what we contemplate in our worship. At Easter, the time of feasting, we contemplate the mystery of Christ's life that is our gateway to eternity: his resurrection. In our singing Alleluia, we are rejoicing that God has shown us, and means to share with us, life that goes beyond death, life that is eternal. This season of Alleluia, the season of Easter, includes the ascension of Our Lord into heaven, which is the entry of our human nature into bliss, and ends with our celebration of Pentecost, which is about the gift of the Holy Spirit, who enables us to live our lives with an eternal perspective.

After this, there is another period of ordinary time, which includes the feasts of the Holy Trinity and of Corpus Christi (marking Christ's gift of himself to us in the Eucharist) and which ends with the feast of Christ the King (marking our celebration of his Lordship of all time). Then the liturgical year begins again with Advent. During the course of the year there are also many feasts of saints, when we celebrate God's gift of himself through the lives of these particular people whose prayers continue to benefit us.

If we go beyond the liturgy section of the library, we find ourselves in the church history section. We believe the Church is the Body of Christ, animated by the Holy Spirit.[8] It follows that in seeking God we will want to find out about the life of the Church through the centuries. Jesus said, "He who has seen me has seen the Father,"[9] and so to see his Body the Church, animated by the Spirit who comes from the Father and from him, is to see God, even if, like Christ on the cross, the Church is so wounded it seems that she has no beauty to make us desire her.[10] These books tell us about the life of the Church.

There is one section of the library that we have still to look at. If we retrace our steps to the philosophy books, we find a

8. 1 Corinthians 12:27
9. John 14:9
10. Isaiah 53:2

doorway in them, as though wisdom were saying to us, "Through here you will find me." Going through this doorway, we find on the left the lives of the saints. Wisdom is found in holiness. "In every generation she passes into holy souls / and makes them friends of God."[11] In these books we can find how these friends of God have come to know and love him. They faced the same struggles that we face and their example guides us in our search for God. They are our friends, who are spiritually present to us today.

The Benedictine order is by no means limited to one school of spirituality. We find help and spiritual nourishment from all God's friends through the ages. Nonetheless, those who have lived the monastic life can give us insights that are especially relevant to us. On the right-hand side are books on the monastic tradition. These tell us about monastic saints, and also about the values and practices that made them what they are. Understanding our tradition by reading these books helps us to find God in our way of life, and so to become holy ourselves.

I have shown you the main sorts of books that we study, but we do not read serious books all the time. There is also recreational reading. If, like Hermione Granger, we spend quite a bit of our time looking at serious books, we might also occasionally be found reading the sort of book she features in![12]

There is the supper bell now. We can get back into the cloister that leads to the refectory by coming out of the library at the end of this section. Let us go to eat now, and after supper I can show you the music room.

---

11. Wisdom 7:27
12. If you don't know what this is, any school child will tell you.

Chapter Fourteen

THE MUSIC ROOM

Our Singing and Its Spiritual Purpose: Harmony with God's Will

Harmony with God's will is the goal of our life in the monastery. That is why we have so many little reminders about what God wants. You will have noticed that at the beginning of supper just now there was a short reading from the Bible. We have this if we have already read the extract from the Rule in the chapter house. It is a way of helping us keep tuned to what God wants for us. There is also grace, as at lunch, though at supper we say grace privately when we finish. Each one is free to leave when he has finished.

If we go to the right outside the refectory and turn right through the door at the end of the cloister and then go up the stairs, we get to the music room. This is the place where we practice singing. When I first came here, my voice was untrained. I was given singing lessons by a good professional singing teacher. I was taught the importance of breathing properly and given exercises to strengthen the muscles that do the singing. This is in miniature the whole of our monastic life.

We need first to breathe properly: that is, to receive the Holy Spirit. Without this God-given inspiration we will not be able to persevere with our monastic life, just as, if I have not breathed deeply enough, I will not be able to keep the note that I am singing. The Bible says Jesus breathed on his disciples and said, "Receive the Holy Spirit."[1] Our spiritual breath comes from him. It enables us to persevere in living our lives in harmony with God's will. Jesus said, "When the Spirit of truth comes, he will guide you into all the truth."[2] This truth is God's will for us. Through the Spirit we are called to be monks and through the Spirit we remain faithful to that calling. The Spirit guides us in our personal prayer, "for we do not know how to pray as we ought, but the Spirit himself intercedes for us with sighs too deep for words."[3]

To be in harmony with God we need the Spirit to know God's will, but we also need to train our own will. This training strengthens the muscles of our will so that we are able to bring it readily into accord with God's will and achieve harmony with it. Monastic life gives this training through the practice of obedience. This is the practice of submitting to what another has decided for us rather than what we happen to feel like doing. Everybody does this to some extent, on pain of being ostracized or unemployed, but monks deliberately practice obedience. In this we follow Jesus, who came not to do his own will but the will of his Father. When he faced an excruciating test of his obedience, he prayed, "not my will, but thine, be done."[4] We will not have suffering of the same order as Our Lord, but we still need to prepare for the ultimate obedience of death. That is why the little crossings of our will that we deliberately undergo are called "mortifications." Through them, we correspond to the teaching of Jesus, who said, "If any man would come after me, let him deny himself and take up his cross daily and follow me. For whoever would save his life will lose it; and whoever loses his life for my sake, he will save it."[5]

---

1. John 20:22
2. John 16:13
3. Romans 8:26
4. Luke 22:42
5. Luke 9:23–24

This is why the Rule of St. Benedict pays such attention to obedience. It tells us to submit to what seems good to another.[6] Neither in principle nor in practice does the abbot give monks tasks because he knows that they are going to be awkward and difficult for these people to do. It is rather a case of monks seeking not to own their will and instead using the abbot's decisions to grow in freedom from self-will. Just as it is possible to be poor in spirit, even if one has quite a lot of resources, by freely and generously using them for the benefit of others, so too can one be obedient in spirit even if (as often happens) one is doing work that is personally agreeable, by allowing the abbot to decide what work is to be done and by doing things with his permission.

It was heartening for me to realize how much progress I could make in singing when I was given lessons about breathing and training the muscles. In the same way, monks can be encouraged that they are following a tried and tested way to bring their lives in harmony with God's will. This harmony of wills ultimately makes it possible for us to be with God in heaven where his will is supreme in all things. Our lessons in will harmony are really lessons in heavenly happiness. When we pray and try to live the petition of the Lord's Prayer, "thy will be done," we are seeking true happiness. The singing that we learn and do on earth is a praise of God that prepares us for the ultimate praise of heaven where we will "sing a new song before the throne."[7]

As well as having music lessons in this room, I also practice my singing here. The choir master kindly records for me the singing that I want to practice, and then I play the tape and sing along with it. By doing this I can get used to keeping my voice at the right pitch. The fact that the choir master's singing is recorded on tape means that he does not have to be here every time I practice, but all the same his example makes it easier for

6. Chapter 72
7. Revelation 14:3

me. Similarly, when we are practicing harmonizing our will with God's, it can help to have the example of a saint: that is, one whose will is established in harmony with God's will. The saint doesn't have to be present in person: a book can be a record of that harmony for us, and reading it can help us to achieve the same harmony. It prepares us to join the saints in the perfect harmony of heaven.

Both here and there, we do not sing alone. My singing lessons are practice for our worship together in church. We sing antiphonally: that is, the two sides of the choir sing alternate verses of the psalms, with a slight pause between verses sung by alternate sides. The sound is like that of breathing in and out, the side that begins being the breathing in and the side that responds the breathing out. It is as though the Body of Christ is breathing in the Holy Spirit and breathing out the spirit of this world. The harmony is an audible sign of the unity I spoke of when we were in the tearoom. It is a unity created by the Holy Spirit. Just as he brought together so many nationalities on the first Pentecost, so he brings together here the monks from many different countries to sing the praise of the Father.

The music that we sing is charged with meaning. First of all it is the meaning of the text. This is either directly or indirectly derived from sacred scripture. Gregorian chant is designed specifically to enhance the meaning of the Latin text, dwelling on syllables that are important and by its rhythm and melody conveying the force and beauty of the inspired words. Sometimes, however, it will take on a life of its own. An example is the extended melody sung on the last syllable of "Alleluia." This is known as a *melisma*. It is the expression of something—in this case joy—that cannot be expressed simply by words and thus breaks out of language as pure song. Something as deep and subtle as our relationship with God cannot be bounded by mere language, and so seeks an expression beyond words in a jubilation of singing. Even music does not fully express it, however, because God is unbounded. Ultimately it hangs in the silence, but the singing gives a setting to that silence as precious metals give a setting to the finest of gems. Just as in our personal prayer we sometimes use words and sometimes are simply silent before this great God of ours, so in our corporate worship there are words and there is silence. The silence perhaps is more expressive since we are communing with the One who transcends all form, and yet the words and the song are not redundant, for we need to be led into his presence.

And the song adds to the words of our prayer. St. Augustine said he who sings, prays twice. Song especially is the expression of the heart. To sing is to make oneself vulnerable. Song is the medium of the lover who opens himself to the mercy of the beloved. In Shakespeare's *Twelfth Night,* Viola is asked what she would do if she loved, and she responds:

> Make me a willow cabin at your gate,
> And call upon my soul within the house;
> Write loyal cantons of contemned love,
> And sing them loud even in the dead of night.[8]

We monks call upon our soul and sing loud to our loving God even in the dead of night. Even if there are times when that love seems to be spurned, our faith, our tradition, and our experience tell us that this is a lover's ruse to draw us on to greater love and confidence.

If we who love God sing to him, does not He who loved us first sing to us? Of that love song, poetry rather than theological doctrine must speak. It is the harmony that is, was, and always will be: the harmony of heaven. It is the harmony that imagina-

---

8. Act 1, Scene 5, lines 268–71

tion has styled "the music of the spheres." Shakespeare wrote of it in the context of love looking at the night sky:

> Look how the floor of heaven
> Is thick inlaid with patens of bright gold.
> There's not the smallest orb which thou behold'st
> But in his motion like an angel sings,
> Still quiring to the young-ey'd cherubins.[9]

Yet, says the poet, this harmony is reserved for "immortal souls"[10] and "whilst this muddy vesture of decay / Doth grossly close it in, we cannot hear it."[11] The implication is that only the one whose will is fixed in harmony with God's in the unshakeable beatitude of heaven is able to hear this harmony.

But is this altogether true? Can faith not tune our hearts to the music of God's will even now? When it listens to God in the silence, does the loving heart hear nothing? To the monk, these are open questions. To be a monk is to listen in the silence. To be a monk is to seek to tune the heart to a melody that is beyond this world. To be a monk is to aim to transcend "this muddy vesture of decay," not by ignoring its existence, for fashioned from clay we are dust and to dust we shall return, but by not allowing it to call the tune. We are not mere clay. An immortal spirit informs our being. Just as a child will recognize and be moved by music played to it before its birth, so we who come "from God, who is our home"[12] know, however obscurely, the melody of our homeland, for

---

9. *Merchant of Venice,* Act 5, Scene 1, lines 58–62

10. Ibid., line 63

11. Ibid., lines 64–65

12. Wordsworth, "Intimations of Immortality from Recollections of Early Childhood," line 66

> Our birth is but a sleep and a forgetting:
> The Soul that rises with us, our life's Star,
> Hath had elsewhere its setting,
> And cometh from afar.[13]

We know the voice of Our Divine Master[14] when he sings to us, for we were made by him, through him, and for him. Our homing instinct is our instinct for harmony, celestial harmony.

What for the individual is expressed by poetry is for the race expressed by Christian doctrine. Humankind "cometh from afar." Man was once unfallen. There seems to be a universal sense of this, in that other traditions apart from the Christian know of a golden age. This was the time of harmony, when the sway of the scepter of the Divine King established the melody of the human heart. It was "very good."[15] Since Man decided to prioritize his own understanding of good and evil over the perfection of divine knowledge,[16] however, disharmony has come into the world. Yet there is a greater harmony that includes this dissonance. Just as in musical composition there is sometimes a chord that seems out of place and jars on the ear, nonetheless, in the context of the whole work, the chord has its place as the means by which beauty of a higher order is introduced, so the disharmony of the fall is the means by which the beautiful music of the Savior is brought into the world which was made through him.[17] To unattuned ears the music was unwelcome. "He came to his own home, and his own people received him not."[18] He said, "To what shall I compare this generation? It is like children sitting in the

---

13. Ibid., lines 59–62
14. John 10:4
15. Genesis 1:31
16. Genesis 3:1–7
17. John 1:10
18. John 1:11

market places and calling to their playmates, 'We piped to you, and you did not dance; we wailed, and you did not mourn.'"[19]

Yet the melody was heard by some, who became "children of God,"[20] dancing to his tune and mourning for the One who was pierced. And it can still be heard. Sacred tradition has not allowed it to fall silent. And thanks to the founder of our monastic congregation, Dom Guéranger, we can hear it with a special richness. He listened for us, listened to the sweet sound of our redemption. And having listened to it through his deep attention to the Christian tradition, he did more. By the inspiration of the Holy Spirit, he determined that such music should not only be listened to in the heart but should also be made among us. Christ is our music, his prayer the audible incarnation of the celestial harmony of the Father. The Church is the Body of Christ and her prayer is his prayer. It is the privilege of the monks and nuns of Dom Guéranger's congregation to make it their lives' priority to pray that prayer, to sing that music, to *be* that music which is the harmony of God among us.

Our music is song, but it is also symbol. Even in its imperfection it is a symbol of willingness to live all our lives in the balance of harmony with God's will. Above all, it is a symbol that speaks to the heart. It makes of the heart a dwelling place for that celestial music which is love. It is our way, the monastic way, of responding to the Apostle's call, "Make love your aim."[21] Our aim is to allow this love to suffuse our hearts and our lives, so that our every encounter in the hills and valleys of our lives is an encounter of love: a love that harmoniously responds to the great harmony that comes from the One, is hidden within all that Providence allows, and is heard with the ears of humble faith.

---

19. Matthew 11:16–17
20. John 1:12
21. 1 Corinthians 14:1

God is One and in him all is perfect harmony. It is the awesome calling of the monk or nun to become attuned to this harmony.

The bells of the abbey church tell it out. They invite us seven times a day to the harmonization of our bodies, our hearts, our minds, and our voices in the worship of the One who made us and loves us as his own. They proclaim the music of his love and invite the song of our response. Soon we shall hear them announcing the last office of the day, Compline, and we shall make that response in the song of our worship together and in the silence of our hearts alone.

Chapter Fifteen

THE CELL

Compline, Staying in One's Cell, and Receiving Inspiration from the Spirit

I nspiration comes especially in the silence. The final service of the day, Compline, marks the beginning of the great silence, which lasts till after Lauds, the second service of the new day. It is in Latin, but for convenience I will give you words from it in English.

It begins in subdued light and there is an examination of conscience. Then the lights come on full and a hymn follows in which we ask for God's protection during the night. One of the psalms sung on some nights picks up this theme. We proclaim our trust in God as we sing, "He who dwells in the shelter of the Most High, / who abides in the shadow of the Almighty, / will say to the LORD, 'My refuge and my fortress; / my God, in whom I trust.'"[1] The Lord responds to this trust: "You will not fear the terror of the night..."[2] He says of the one who trusts him, " I will protect him, because he knows my name. / When he calls to me, I will answer him; / I will be with him in trouble."[3] After the psalmody we turn to face the altar and once more show our trust

---

1. Psalm 91:1–2
2. Psalm 91:5
3. Psalm 91:14–15

in God by echoing in song the words of Our Lord on the cross: "Into your hands, Lord, I commend my spirit,"[4] confident that God has redeemed us. This, the end of the day, is a kind of rehearsal for the end of our life when we will finally give our spirit into God's hands. This is made clear by our singing of the canticle of Simeon, the old man who took the baby Jesus in his arms in the temple.[5] It had been revealed to him by the Holy Spirit that he would not die before he had seen the Christ.[6] When he was granted this privilege, he was ready to die because he knew God's saving work had been accomplished. In faith we too know God's saving work and show our own readiness to give our lives back to him whenever he might choose. And so we make our own the words of Simeon:

> "Lord, now lettest thou thy servant depart in peace,
>   according to thy word;
> for mine eyes have seen thy salvation
>   which thou hast prepared in the presence of all peoples,
> a light for revelation to the Gentiles
>   and for glory to thy people Israel."[7]

After the concluding prayer for Compline, we turn to the east and look up to the statue of Our Lady above the high altar. She is our patron, and the final song of our day is addressed to her. We sing different antiphons according to the season, but the ordinary one, which you hear today, begins "Hail Holy Queen, Mother of mercy; hail our life, our sweetness, and our hope!" She is our hope because from her the Savior of the world was born. We are about to call this to mind silently in the Angelus, the

---

4. Luke 23:46
5. Luke 2:28
6. Luke 2:26
7. Luke 2:29–32

prayer that remembers Mary's agreement to this great calling. First, though, the abbot sprinkles us with holy water, which is our final prayer for protection during the night.

Then, as the light fades, the final sound of our worship before the great silence rings out: the Angelus bell. And silently, in our hearts, we turn to Mary and say, "Pray for us, O Holy Mother of God, that we may be made worthy of the promises of Christ." These promises are mysterious because they are about things that eye has not seen nor ear heard,[8] but there is one kind of human promise that gives us an idea of them. It too is associated with the ringing of church bells. It is the promise of marriage. The exchange of promises in a wedding is a most heart-touching moment. I have never exchanged such promises myself, but I have witnessed many weddings just feet away from the couples. It is a time of intense personal emotion. This can be seen on the faces of the spouses, and they talk about it afterward, often tearfully. One bride wrote afterward that she felt, as the vows were made, the ground under her feet changing from quicksand to granite.

So it is with us with the promises of Christ, which he makes to his bride, the Church. I want to clear up a little ambiguity at this point. All of us in the monastery are male, but collectively, as the Church, we are female. And through his gospel the Lord makes us solemn promises. One such promise speaks especially of our personal encounter with God, the encounter that we live especially in the privacy of our cells. It is in St. John's Gospel: "If a man loves me, he will keep my word, and my Father will love him, and we will come and make our home with him."[9]

This is an awesome promise. It involves everything. Everything belongs to God. The earth and its fullness are the LORD's,[10] says the scripture, but I first learned this from an Arab taxi driver. I

---

8. 1 Corinthians 2:9
9. John 14:23
10. Psalm 24:1

wanted to pay him less than what he was asking. When he refused the money I offered, I said, "Take it, it is yours." "No," he replied, "it belongs to God." As St. Paul said to the Athenians, "In him we live and move and have our being."[11] Each person as well as each thing is held in being by God. So if God makes his home with us, we can be alone in our cells and yet have no separation from anyone or anything. If God is in our heart, every person is there also because everyone exists only in God. If God is in our heart, all creation is there also, because all of it too exists only in God. God's presence in our hearts brings a deep intimacy with all of humanity and with the sea and the stars too. But to have God making his home with us is not just communion with all of creation, it also communion with him. It means sharing his joy, his bliss. Just as spouses share each other's joy, so the one with whom God makes his home shares his joy. And happily, unlike spouses, God is joyful all the time. If he is living with us, we can always be happy for him because he is always happy. So the cell is a place of happiness. And it is also a place of peace. The Lord says, "My peace I give to you; not as the world gives do I give to you."[12] That peace can coexist with outward troubles that do not take it away, as it did for Our Lord as he faced his suffering and death.

We get to enjoy the wonder of God making his home with us by following what Our Lord says: "If a man loves me, he will keep my word."[13] It is clear from the scriptural context that this word is essentially the injunction given in the previous chapter of the Gospel to love one another even as Our Lord has loved us.[14] This injunction is repeated in the chapter that follows.[15]

---

11. Acts 17:28
12. John 14:27
13. John 14:23
14. John 13:34
15. John 15:12

Through the Holy Spirit, we love one another with Christ's love. "The Holy Spirit" says the Lord, "will teach you all things."[16] A good teacher guides and motivates. So does the Holy Spirit. First he places the source of love at the center of our lives. St. Paul says, "No one can say 'Jesus is Lord' except by the Holy Spirit."[17] The Spirit leads us to Jesus and makes him Our Lord. The Spirit enkindles love of the Lord in us, the love by which we are motivated to keep his word. We keep his word by seeing and loving him in others, especially those who are strangers or who are hungry, thirsty, naked, sick, or imprisoned, says the Gospel of St. Matthew;[18] and the Rule of St. Benedict says we should see and love Christ especially in the abbot.[19] But we see and love the Lord in all humanity, for he has taken on our humanity. And the Holy Spirit, who will teach us all things, guides us by his promptings as to what we do when. His inspiration gives us a surer direction than our likes and dislikes. Our likes are not a sufficient guide. It is the same as with food. Just as following our likes will not necessarily give us a healthy and balanced diet, so in loving others we are prompted to go beyond our likes. Our dislikes are not a barrier to loving because we can love with God's love, the Holy Spirit, by praying for the people concerned. In the Holy Spirit, God gives us everything we need to prepare to welcome him as a guest. We can welcome him as a guest in our cells and our hearts because, thanks to his Spirit, all of humanity finds a place in our hearts.

So as the bells ring out to mark night and its silence—and in all our nights, whatever form they may take—we open our hearts to the prompting of the Spirit, so that he may lead us to what has

---

16. John 14:26
17. 1 Corinthians 12:3
18. Matthew 25:31–46
19. Rule of St. Benedict, Chapter 2

been promised, and we ask the holy Mother of God to pray for us that we may be made worthy of the promises of Christ.

Then we go to our cells. A monk's cell is the most character-istic place for him to be. Even before monasteries as we now know them came to be, monks would live in a cell. There is an old monastic tradition that if you go to your cell, your cell will teach you everything. This is like saying "know yourself" for it is in the cell that we are most who we are. Without any distractions, or anyone to make an impression on, we are encouraged to be who we truly are and to go more deeply into our heart, where the Uncreated God lives. This is where we find his peace, the peace the world cannot give.[20] It is the opposite movement from that anxious agitation that seeks to stamp a selfish claim onto the pass-ing things of this world. This sort of activity may give the illusion of one's being in the midst of reality, but it is actually the pursuit of a fantasy: that around the bundle of egotistic desires that we mistake for our true self, we can construct a true life independent of God. This pursuit belongs to time, which is the mere husk of eternity. The cell lacks the multifarious apparatus of the world for engaging egotistic desires, and here these desires can be seen for what they are: distractions from the real business of being open to that eternal love ever seeking to engage us from the core of our being. And yet in the cell as we open our hearts to God, we are in a certain sense opening all of humanity to God. Nothing and no one is neglected in God.

The word *cell* may seem to have negative connotations of cus-tody and confinement. But we can look at it more positively. The cell is where the bee makes and stores honey. It is a creative place. It is the place where God comes and makes his home with us. It is the place where the sweet honey of devotion is made. Our Lord said, "When you pray, go into your room and shut the door and pray to your Father who is in secret; and your Father who sees in

---

20. John 14:27

secret will reward you."[21] It is in hiddenness that prayer can be most sincere, since there is no one to act in front of. This hiddenness is a continuation of the hiddenness of the public prayer, where our individuality is hidden behind the set and common form of the prayer. By following this, we seek to leave behind the posturing of the self. In our private prayer and reflection we also want to avoid this. So we stay in our cells.

And even if this does have connotations of custody and confinement, they need not be bad. Our angels keep guard over us and if our cells associate us with those who are held prisoner, then maybe we can learn from them. Before I came to live here, I had the privilege of working in a prison as a chaplain. There I met people who were deprived, almost by definition, of social esteem and of the usual opportunities for distraction. In some cases this enabled them to see their need of God's mercy better than many people on the outside. I saw this in many circumstances, but one spoke to me particularly because of its closeness to the lives of monks. This was the group of prisoners who lived together on a dedicated wing and followed a drug rehabilitation program. Their life as a group made them like monks in a monastery because they were seeking God's mercy together. I say they were seeking God's mercy because they were following the 12-step program first pioneered by Alcoholic Anonymous. Although AA allows a wide range of ways of describing what goes on in its program, it is essentially founded on the Christian understanding that spiritual healing is found through accepting our need for God's mercy.

This program begins with a recognition of powerlessness, that we cannot sort everything out with the supposed strength of our own ego. It moves to the recognition of a higher power (God) and a turning over of one's life to that power. The next step is to look at one's life and failings fearlessly and then to share this with

---

21. Matthew 6:6

God and another person. There are further steps, but this is as far as this particular prison program went. As a chaplain, I shared in the group-therapy sessions and in the physical training in the gym. I also listened as individuals shared their moral accounting of their lives. I witnessed the community that was built up from their shared vulnerability. In effect, they were living out the monastic quest, which the one who comes here to be a monk asks to share with us. We ask, "What do you seek?" and he replies, "God's mercy and fellowship with you."

I also witnessed the finding of God's mercy in the confinement of a prison cell. For example, there was a prisoner in solitary confinement to whom the Lord spoke through a gospel passage. This led finally to his being baptized into the Church during the Easter Vigil Mass. He wept as he became an adopted child of God, having found the mercy of God.

For my last day in the prison—I was leaving to come here—the prisoners wanted to sing a favorite hymn of mine. I asked them to sing St. Thomas Aquinas's *"Adoro Te Devote."* They sang it, ending with the words *"Peto quod petivit latro penitens"*—"I seek what the penitent thief sought." On the cross, next to Our Lord, this thief asked, "Jesus, remember me when you come in your kingly power."[22] He asked for mercy. This is exactly what we ask for as monks. That day in the prison I was aware that in my calling as a monk I was sharing with the penitent thief and the convicted prisoners there that deep cry of the human heart, "Lord, have mercy."

God is all mercy, and in my cell I seek to be still in the presence of the Merciful One, to drink from the fountain of his mercy. I aim to open myself to the inspiration of his Spirit, which speaks to me of mercy, redemption, and love. I seek to be in his presence, simply happy to be with him as with a friend. From my

---

22. Luke 23:42

window I can see the goods of the world being shipped in and out of Southampton, and I can see the naval stronghold of Portsmouth, but my hope is not in the goods of this world nor in its strength, but in my Lord who loved me and gave himself up for me. While you go to sleep in the guesthouse, I go to sleep in my cell and say,

> Thou hast put more joy in my heart
>> than they have when their grain and wine abound.

> In peace I will both lie down and sleep;
>> for thou alone, O Lord, makest me dwell in safety.[23]

---

23. Psalm 4:7–8

Chapter Sixteen

THE CHURCH

The Mystery of God, Vigils, Lauds, and Mass

Mystery is at the heart of our life here. I can tell you about the abbey church, but I will not be able to describe the One whose home it is. He is beyond all we can say. All I can do is point to some symbols which speak of him here in this church. When I have done that, I will also say something about the offices of Vigils and Lauds, which you already attended here before breakfast, and something about Mass, which we celebrate daily at nine o'clock in the morning. One phrase used for the celebration of Mass is "the sacred mysteries" and, indeed, the Mass makes present the mystery of God; however, as with the other worship and, indeed, all expressions of the ineffable, what channels the mystery also veils it. The church is a place where we worship and we pray; above all it is a place where we are in the presence of a mystery, the mystery of God.

We are very blessed to have a monastic church whose architect was a monk, Dom Paul Bellot. To employ an architect, however good, outside the monastic family is inevitably to be involved in a negotiation of visions. This church, by contrast, is the direct expression of a monastic vision. We get some idea of what that vision is by what Dom Bellot himself said about how art works: "True art builds on a foundation of good sense and simplicity; it grows up in silence and humility; it is the fruit of the whole spirit and heart of man. The Gospel tells us that Paradise is for those who are like children; and art is like a door opened upon the achievements and harmonies of blessed eternity…"[1] I believe that this abbey church at Quarr is a fulfillment of Dom Bellot's vision of true art: it does indeed open a door upon the achievements and harmonies of blessed eternity.

It does this first of all by being a place of peace. Dom Bellot saw a church as a place of separation from what agitates. A church needs to suggest peace in its proportions. This church does just that, though we believe that the impression of peace that so many people receive here is more than simply the effect of outstanding architecture. This church is the home of the Prince of Peace, and his presence is evoked here everyday in worship and in prayer. It may be too, as I said at the beginning of your visit, that the holiness of this church is connected with the worship of those monks who worshipped before us on this site, the ruins of whose monastery you saw yesterday. Certainly this peace is something that is experienced again and again by people coming to this church. Some are moved to tears. It is an impression that does not cease with time. The monk I told you about—who said shortly before his death, after fifty years here, "Fancy spending the rest of your life in church!"—also reported feeling the spiritual aura of this church every time he came in here. I feel it myself. It is something I am drawn back to if I am away. I cannot easily ignore it. I came into the church once in a hurry simply to look for someone, and I felt gently rebuked: it was not appropriate to rush into such a majestic presence. The Prince of Peace is indeed here.

---

1. Quoted by Sister Mary Totah, OSB, the Introduction, in *The Spirit of Solesmes,* by Dom Prosper Gueranger, Abbess Cecile Bruyere, and Dom Paul Delatte, ed. Sister Mary Totah, OSB (Tunbridge Wells, UK: Burns & Oates / Petersham, MA: St. Bede's Publichations, 1997), 39.

This church is a place of peace and it is also a place of light. The Prince of Peace is the light of the world,[2] and the architect of the church wanted to convey this truth. He set himself to make the sun dance before it came into the church, and indeed it does. You will notice that the pattern of light here is hardly ever the same. At times the wind moving the clouds and the trees puts the light into continual movement. God's Holy Spirit moves where he wills,[3] and the light in the church is a symbol that every encounter with God is wonderfully new. The light changes moment by moment and also hour by hour. The bright light of the dawn, coming through the windows at the east beyond the sanctuary, speaks of the beginning of the spiritual life: that first brightness that reevaluates our whole life. The light of midday, coming through the southern windows where the trees are, speak of the changes of our life and the labor of the day. The light of evening, coming from the west, is stiller and quieter. There is a more mellow feeling to it. Since the windows toward the west are very low, there are no sudden changes to the light. This reflects the evening of our life when we are steadier in our feelings and live not so much by the consolation of the felt presence of light as by faith. It is a beautiful thing to pray in the church as it gets dark. As the light outside peacefully fades, the candle in the sanctuary lamp seems to become brighter. Our faith does not need great shafts of illumination to say simply, "Jesus is here."

The light in the church speaks to us of him and so does the structure. It is deliberately constructed to speak of our journey to him. If you come in at the back, you will notice that this part of the church is lower than the rest. This indicates and facilitates the separation from the world of the monks worshipping in the choir. Passersby can come in and see what is going on, but there is a degree of protection for those in the choir from the distraction of

2. John 8:12
3. John 3:8

what is passing. Dimly lit and on a lower level, it is not the real business that we are about.

Our real business is indicated by the monks' choir. Its joyful simplicity occupies the largest area of the church, just as our singing of the Divine Office is the largest part of our work. It is the sanctuary, however, that draws the attention. It is the focus of the church. The emphasis is on the presence and sacrifice of Christ, denoted respectively by the tabernacle and the altar. The eye is drawn to the hanging tabernacle above the altar where the Blessed Sacrament is reserved: Jesus makes his home here. And looking down from the east wall, as if to say, "Do whatever he tells you,"[4] is Mary, his mother, unobtrusively praying for and welcoming us. The church is the ideal place to pray because everything is drawn to him. The glow in the sanctuary lamp and in the heart tells us that he is there. And the church tells us of the effect of coming to him. As we approach the sanctuary, the warmth of the color of the bricks increases and the light becomes stronger. He is the light of the world.[5] When we are in the church—with Christ—we can look up and, seeing the ceiling of the sanctuary, have a sense of the celestial that we reach through him. The tower seems to be made of bricks thrown into the air. To do this with bricks seems impossible. Indeed, it is said that when the time came for the scaffolding used to construct the tower to be taken down, the workmen who had built it refused to do so, and the architect had to demonstrate the confidence of his convictions by doing it himself. As it is for the bricks, so it is for us: we are clay,[6] like the bricks, and weighed down by our belonging to the earth, yet Christ takes us up to heaven and makes of us something beautiful.

He does this by our participation in his life. We participate in it by prayer and love of others. Here, that is centered on our cele-

---

4. John 2:5
5. John 8:12
6. Genesis 2:7

bration of the liturgy—the Divine Office and the Mass—and our fraternal good will toward each other and all those in our lives. I will take you through the liturgy of the morning in a moment, but first, as we are thinking about the church, let me tell you a little about a special day in our calendar: October twelfth. This is the anniversary of the dedication of our church, and we keep this as a major solemnity—the highest grade of feast. On a day like this, we follow the Sunday timetable, without work other than what needs to be done (such as cooking meals). The church is beautifully decorated with candles encircled by wreaths of yew along the walls. Our worship celebrates the church as a place of the presence of God, and reminds us that we too are temples of the Holy Spirit.

Today, the liturgy was more ordinary. We started with Vigils at half past five, with the versicle, "LORD, open my lips."[7] This recognizes that this office is, like all our worship, the work of the Lord. "We do not know how to pray as we ought, but the Spirit Himself intercedes for us."[8] The fact that we worship at all is a gift of God, but we nonetheless bring our part. The name *Vigils* suggests the spiritual attitude that we seek to cultivate. We are in search of an awakening. This is true in the literal sense—at this time of morning we are likely to be struggling to control sleepy thoughts—but also symbolically. We want to awaken from the dream that the things of time and space are the defining reality. They are not. Eternity is the reality by which time and space are defined. Heaven is more real than earth. Characteristic of this office are the psalms that tell the story of the people of God, the exodus from Egypt to the promised land. This is an image of our own awakening, our exodus from slavery to the passing things of time, to the freedom of seeking "the things that are above, where Christ is, seated at the right hand of God."[9]

---

7. Psalm 51:15
8. Romans 8:26
9. Colossians 3:1

Vigils is also called the "Office of Readings." This indicates the concomitant of awakening: listening. Faith comes by hearing.[10] We could just scan our eyes over the texts silently instead of hearing them read, but it would not be the same. The readings make a more vital impact on the heart if they are heard. The human voice is a more intimate instrument than the written word. There are two readings: one is from scripture and the other is from the fathers of the Church. These give us respectively God's word and reflection upon it, an opportunity to hear, and to take what we hear to heart.

After Vigils there is a time of about three-quarters of an hour until Lauds at seven o'clock. We can use the time for having breakfast, but it is also a good time for silent prayer in the church. Like Vigils, Lauds begins with an acknowledgment that it is the Lord who does the work. The one leading the worship sings, "O God come to my assistance" and the choir responds, "Lord, make haste to help me."[11] These words from the psalms are a traditional monastic prayer for help in all circumstances. Again, the name of the office suggests the spiritual attitude we want to cultivate. *Lauds* means "praise." Having, as it were, awakened to the Lord and listened to him, we know him somewhat and so there is a love for him that wants to praise him. This attitude is essential to spiritual life. In one sense, it is simple realism. It recognizes God as who he is, in all his wonder and majesty. And because of God's gracious love for us, he waits to act in our world until we give him permission. Praise gives him that permission by acknowledging his majesty and thus letting him be, for us, who he is. Praise is therefore a good preparation for any prayer of intercession, such as for healing. Praise gives God the green light to enter our lives.

Perhaps the most potent symbol of that entry is light. When we seek truth, we talk about bringing light to bear on a matter;

---

10. Romans 10:17
11. Psalm 40:13

Jesus called himself the light of the world.[12] Light therefore denotes God's manifestation. This is celebrated particularly in the climax of Lauds, the Benedictus, the canticle sung by Zechariah, who, filled with the Holy Spirit, announces the epoch that his prophet son will usher in, a time "when the day shall dawn upon us from on high / to give light to those who sit in darkness and in the shadow of death, / to guide our feet into the way of peace."[13] Light is also a symbol of life, by contrast with the shadow of death that the Savior comes to dispel. He came that we might have life and have it abundantly.[14] And Lauds happens at the time of dawning, sometimes approximately, sometimes exactly. The beginning of the day says the same thing as our worship: light is coming into our world.

The time between Lauds and Mass lasts about an hour and a half. We normally use it for *lectio divina:* that is, as I mentioned to you before, spiritual reading or prayerful reflection on sacred writing. Having together listened to and praised God, we give him the opportunity to speak to us individually through the written word.

Mass is the climactic point of our worship. It is also called the *Eucharist,* and this gives an idea of the spiritual attitude associated with it: in Greek it means "thanksgiving." As I said when we were speaking of Vespers, thanksgiving is the essence of spiritual life. In the Mass, we thank God for everything, but above all for the gift of Jesus, and his sacrifice of himself for our redemption. And we also offer this sacrifice: the Mass is sometimes called the Holy Sacrifice. In making this offering, we also offer *ourselves* with him to be transformed. This is simply an offering of our time, our presence, and our attention.

The first part of the Mass is called the Liturgy of the Word and in it, having acknowledged our need of God's mercy and collected our thoughts in prayer, we listen to scripture being read

---

12. John 8:12
13. Luke 1:68–79, here 78–79.
14. John 10:10

and, if it is a Sunday or a major feast, preaching. Then, at the start
of the second part of the Mass, the Liturgy of the Eucharist, we
offer ourselves symbolically in the Offertory Procession, in which
a couple of us bring up the bread and wine to the altar. As we
walk up to the altar in this church, the colors of the bricks
becoming warmer and the light becoming brighter symbolize our
transformation in Christ. As we allow him to suffuse our lives,
our love becomes warmer and our minds become enlightened.

The main prayer of the Mass, the Eucharistic Prayer, trans-
forms the bread and wine, tokens of our gift of self, into the Body
and Blood of Christ. A bell rings out to mark this. This transformation becomes a transformation of ourselves. When we receive
communion, Jesus comes to live in us. We seek to be like St. Paul,
who said, "It is no longer I who live, but Christ who lives in
me."[15] This communion is the partaking of a sacred meal that
(like our eating in the refectory, but more explicitly) anticipates
the eschatological banquet, that final rejoicing in heaven that we
reflected on when we were talking about our eating arrangements.

We privately give thanks for so great a presence within us,
One that we hope will shine as light from our eyes, as love and
blessing for all whom we encounter. Then we sing the short office
of Terce, which normally takes the form of part of a psalm reflecting on and giving thanks for God's revelation of himself.[16] The
Mass ends with a prayer and a blessing; the dismissal enjoins us
to "Go in peace" or "to love and serve the Lord." This directs us
to what our incorporation in Christ in the Mass and indeed in all
the liturgy means: peace with and service of others. Above all for
us in the monastery, this means peace with and service of our
brothers here, but we do not forget our friends and our families.
We also acknowledge our social responsibilities. It may seem that

---

15. Galatians 2:20
16. Psalm 119

being apart in a monastery makes us less part of the society around us than others, but in some ways the opposite is true. Our prayer links us to all people, because God holds all in being. And people often bring their concerns and difficulties to a monastery and to monks precisely because we live somewhat apart and can offer a perspective that is not so caught up in the web of interests that crisscrosses society. In our prayer and in such influence as we have on others, we seek the kingdom of God: his will and his justice, for it is only in the context of this will and this justice that peace will flourish. They are both the outflowing and the condition of the liturgy. The Gospel tells us, "If you are offering your gift at the altar, and there remember that your brother has something against you, leave your gift there before the altar and go; first be reconciled to your brother, and then come and offer your gift."[17] The "Sign of Peace" that we give during the Mass is a demonstration of the importance of justice and peace for our eucharistic worship. Being one with the Lord means being one with the least of his brethren, such as those who suffer and die before they are big enough even to be born. Our offering of ourselves to God in the Mass is an offering of ourselves also for others, since God is love. This offering is finding true life. Our Lord has said to us, "Whoever loses his life for my sake, he will save it."[18] God is never outdone in generosity.

Hear the bell ringing? It is time to prepare for the Mass now, but before we go I would like you to take one last look at the church. Do you see how everything in the church draws the attention to the tabernacle hanging above the altar where Jesus is? We seek to be like this church, with everything in us directed to Our Lord. This building helps us. I'll let you stay for a few minutes here after the Mass so that you can experience this, and then I'll come to take you on the final stages of our tour.

---

17. Matthew 5:23–24
18. Luke 9:24

Chapter Seventeen

THE CEMETERY

Death, and Those Who Have Gone Before Us

Death is the final seal of our monastic life. Traditionally, the important thing is to die "in the habit." Even kings would sometimes join a monastery toward the end of their lives so as to accomplish this. Perseverance to the end is an essential part of our life. Of other callings—even other religious callings, such as being a bishop—we say that someone served in this capacity for so many years, and then retired. Monks do not retire, they are buried. That does not mean that the old and frail have to come to every office in the church right up to the moment of their death; this would be an inhuman demand. But if they do not come to everything—or indeed to anything—it is because they have permission not to come, on account of their frailty. They do not retire from what is most essential about being a monk: obedience. Even in not attending worship in the church, they are obeying the abbot.

The final obedience, however, is not to the abbot but directly to God, who calls us when he wills. It is an obedience required of everyone, but a monk specializes in preparing for it. Like the final end of the world we pass our days in, we do not know the hour of it; we can only "take heed, watch, and pray."[1] As I hope I

---

1. Mark 13:32–33

have been able to show you in the course of our tour, a monk is one who takes heed of the things of eternity, one who watches and prays. But we cannot say absolutely that a man is a monk until he has persevered in watching and praying until the end. "Blessed are those servants whom the master finds awake when he comes."[2] Being awake is not a matter of not taking rest that we need: it is, like Vigils, being awake from the dream that the things of time and space are the defining reality, being awake to eternity, to the promise of heaven. Let us go now to the cemetery, and I shall tell you a little about some of those who were awake till the end, who proved themselves truly monks.

We leave the church now by the west door. More usually we monks go out of the church by the north door leading into the cloister, but this is the door that our mortal remains are taken through at the accomplishment of our monastic life. God willing, one day the Mass that has just been celebrated will be my funeral Mass. My body will be carried through this door, and the procession will turn left outside the church, where we are going now, and then left again through these gates and down alongside the church to the cemetery on the right hand side. Coming through the gate now we see before us the graves of accomplished monks, our predecessors and exemplars.

Here is the French monk I told you about who told me how to scythe. You could tell he was French because he always pursed his lips when taking a piece of cheese. Here is the monk who joined the monastery late in life, having been a very distinguished professor of mathematics. He had a gentleness and courtesy that was rooted in the supernatural. This is a monk who persevered in coming to office in the church even when the infirmity of age had almost bent him double and he could hardly move except by shuffling. This is a grave that is visited even by people who never

---

2. Luke 12:37

met the monk buried here. He was a guest master for a long time and had a great influence on guests, one of whom wrote a book about him that sold very well: Tony Hendra, author of *Father Joe*. People who have read it ask to see Father Joe's grave. Next to it is the grave of a much-loved prior. This monk had an extraordinary openness to people, and many with beliefs very different from those of the Catholic Church counted him their friend.

Each monk buried here has his own story of how God called him, first to the monastery to prepare for meeting him, and then to himself at the accomplishment of his monastic life. One of them came to the monastery as a result of asking a ticket clerk at Waterloo station in London to give him a day return ticket to somewhere nice for a day out. The clerk sensibly sold him a ticket to the Isle of Wight, where he found Quarr Abbey and decided this was where he must live all his days.

The monks who have probably had the most influence on our monastery have been its abbots. There are two of them here whom I knew personally. One was an aeronautical engineer. His engineering skills were very useful in stabilizing the church when cracks began to appear, but it was his contemplative spirit that was his greatest contribution to the monastery. "If only you knew," he would say, "the gift of God."[3] The other one was abbot when I first visited the monastery. I will never forget the radiance with which he welcomed guests. I knew intuitively that here was someone who really understood how to live life. He started his monastic life at another monastery, and I also spent some time there before coming to Quarr Abbey for good.

Whatever they achieved in their lives, the graves of these monks are marked simply by a stone cross inscribed with their name and the date of their death. Their work does not need to be

---

3. John 4:10

advertised. God knows the intentions that filled their hearts, and they are with him now.

But we remember them. And we remember them in a particular way on November second, All Souls Day, a day on which prayers are said for departed souls. After the Mass that morning we come in procession down to the cemetery, and there special prayers are said for the repose of the souls of those buried here. They are still our brothers and we give them the help of our intercession. We believe that we receive help from them too. In fact, although we come here on All Souls Day, we are also specially linked with them the day before, All Saints Day. On this day we celebrate the happiness of all those in heaven, not just those who are formally canonized as saints by the Church. It is reasonable to hope that our brothers whose mortal remains lie here are among them, and that their prayers help us. Death does not end our spiritual brotherhood. Indeed, we feel that even the hundreds of years that separate us from the monks of old Quarr do not stop us having a spiritual link with them. A soul who is with God shares his ability to touch peoples of all epochs.

These monks who have died have left this world to enter eternity and participate in the freedom of God, but we who are still alive share something of their happy state through our profession as monks. When a monk makes his solemn profession, he gives away any possessions he might have and promises obedience to his abbot. St. Benedict says that when a monk has taken his vows definitively, not even his own body is at his disposal.[4] Having no property of his own and (since another decides what he is to do) no will of his own, he is as one who is already dead. All of us have to hand back to God our stewardship of our possessions and ourselves when we die; monks do so in anticipation of death when they commit themselves to the monastic life. In

---

4. Rule of St. Benedict, Chapter 58

doing this we seek to belong to God like those who have given up their selves to him in the finality of death. Living according to our vows gives us a freedom from egotistical self-will and petty selfishness. The partial and limited life of the self is exchanged for the unbounded life of God.

This exchange is not the privilege of monks alone. It is in fact what all Christians receive at least in germ at their baptism. St. Paul explains this, saying, "All of us who have been baptized into Christ Jesus were baptized into his death. We were buried therefore with him by baptism into death, so that as Christ was raised from the dead by the glory of the Father, we too might walk in newness of life."[5] When a monk makes his solemn profession, he is simply owning in an explicit way the fact of his Christian baptism. The water of baptism is at one and the same time a symbol of death (to go under the water is to die) and of life (water is necessary for life). Baptism enacts the death of selfishness and the beginning of new life that we have in following the will of God as a member of Christ's Body. Through it we belong to Jesus, who died and rose again, but as the anointing with the oil of catechumens during baptism of babies signifies, we still have to learn his ways. Baptism received as an infant is a seed that needs to be nurtured for it to grow. An adult receiving baptism can understand it as a conscious and deliberate dying to selfishness and living for God, but those of us who have been baptized as babies need to make explicit in our lives the meaning of baptism. Monastic life does this par excellence.

To be a monk is to lay claim to the promise expressed by St. Paul:

> If we have been united with him in a death like his, we
> shall certainly be united with him in a resurrection like
> his. We know that our old self was crucified with him so

5. Romans 6:3–4

that the sinful body might be destroyed, and we might no longer be enslaved to sin. For he who has died is freed from sin. But if we have died with Christ, we believe that we shall also live with him. For we know that Christ being raised from the dead will never die again; death no longer has dominion over him. The death he died he died to sin, once for all, but the life he lives he lives to God.[6]

This life with Christ is a gift of God, but we need to own it by considering ourselves "dead to sin and alive to God in Christ Jesus."[7] Through faith we seek to refuse what is not life giving and to trust God through, with, and in Jesus.

We need to live this out day by day. Our monastic life is the living out of our baptism. Basically, it has two elements. The first is prayer, which is being "alive to God in Christ Jesus." Our prayer has many forms: for example, prayer together in the church, personal prayer, prayerful spiritual reading, and prayerful attemps to align ourselves with God by doing his will, whether in our work or in our conversation with others. The other element is traditionally called "mortification." That includes being "dead to sin" but it extends to dying to self, wherever we may find self or selfishness. It is to die to self, or escape selfishness, that we undertake obedience. As long as it is not actually sinful, it does not matter so much what we are doing as long as it does not come from our own self. Living under obedience means we do what we do because we have been asked to do it, or because it is the tradition of the house, or, at least, because we have permission to do it. This has the goal of transcending our own self, and, as Our Lord promised, losing our life for his sake that we may find it.[8]

---

6. Romans 6:5–10
7. Romans 6:11
8. Matthew 10:39

Another way of looking at these two elements, being alive to God and dead to sin, is to see them as being the path to eternity and refusing to allow ourselves to be trapped into identifying our life's purpose with that which passes. Our eternity with God is what matters, not what comes and passes. That is why the monastic tradition fosters an awareness of death. To get a healthy perspective on life, we need to understand that we irrevocably shall leave what passes and enter eternity where only our relationship with God matters. And so the Rule of St. Benedict says that we should have death before our eyes daily.[9] This is not something morbid. Rather it is the joyful conviction that our life leads to something fuller and greater. If it has a minatory aspect, it is to warn us that we are not to spend our lives in trivial pre-occupations: our lives are much too important for that.

Nature helps us to keep this injunction of the Rule. When we come down to the cemetery here on All Souls Day, it is autumn. The falling leaves remind us that we too will die as those whom we remember here have died. Each onset of winter speaks of our departure from this life. The bare trees that I see from the window of my cell evoke the skeletal remains that in all probability will be all that is left of my body in less time than it has spent in this world to date. Spring, when it comes, is a pledge of that new life that we look to enjoy eternally. It tells of more than this, however. It is also the image of that life here and now, which is freed from all selfish warpings, the life that is lived for God and not for some partial advantage in the futile struggle to lay hold of the passing things of this world. This is a life which is not dominated by fear—"to die is gain"[10]—and which enjoys "the glorious liberty of the children of God,"[11] the liberty of not being anxious because

9. Chapter 4
10. Philippians 1:21
11. Romans 8:21

"we know that in everything God works for good with those who love him, who are called according to his purpose."[12]

Often people who have this life in its fullness have undergone some identifiable experience when they have already died as far as hopes and expectations of this world are concerned. St. Teresa of Avila had the experience of her grave literally being dug while she was still alive.[13] It was thought that her illness was so obviously leading to death that preparations needed to be made. Surviving, she went on to live a different kind of life: a life that knows in the heart that all in this world is passing and that all that matters is the degree to which we experience the indwelling of God, who is love. In order to help people gain this supremely valuable kind of life, God allows his friends to have taken away from them things to which they have attached expectations, things which comfort their hearts. He knows that those who mourn are blessed, for they shall be comforted.[14] Hence, even though deprivations may grieve his friends in the short term, in the long term these deprivations make possible a sharing of life from his perspective, which is unboundedly joyful. The deprivation may be an illness or a bereavement, which are the common lot of humankind, but a monk is also liable to have things taken away from him by virtue of his promise to obey the abbot. In principle this could include anything he uses, and in practice it will include a changing of what he does. The purpose of these changes, even—or perhaps particularly—when they are painful for the monk concerned, is the same as the loving purpose of God: to give true life.

St. John of the Cross, who was Teresa of Avila's friend, wrote about spiritual life in terms of undergoing deathlike deprivations that open the soul to new life. These he called "dark nights." The

---

12. Romans 8:28
13. *Life of St. Teresa,* Chapter 5
14. Matthew 5:4

night comes about because the soul is drawn away from its normal source of stimulation to find its life in God. Not having what it is used to having, its subjective experience is one of darkness though in fact it is in the presence of uncreated light. The dark night of the senses is the experience of leaving behind a life that draws its sustenance from the things of this world to be oriented instead toward the things of God. The dark night of the spirit is the experience of leaving behind the things of God for the sake of God himself: it is exchanging the gifts for the Giver. These nights are not simply having a difficult patch in one's life because of a change in what is available for one's comfort. They are a radical transformation of the soul that comes about as a concomitant of a life consistently fed by the theological virtues of faith, hope, and love. Faith gives the intelligence what is beyond the reach of the mind, hope gives a memory that cherishes what no experience has provided, and love gives the will what it would never have the strength to offer on its own. The virtues are called "theological" because they are spiritual gifts of God leading us to him, not good habits that can be acquired through one's own efforts (as, for example, the habit of turning up on time for things). They are received in the context of a life that is lived in radical dependence on God. This sense that we need to receive all of life from God is at the heart of Christian spirituality. It is summed up by the first Beatitude, "Blessed are the poor in spirit, for theirs is the kingdom of heaven."[15] The Benedictine spiritual tradition guides us into this radical dependence on God by its emphasis on humility. Our Rule refers us to the psalm that says, "I have calmed and quieted my soul, / like a child quieted at its mother's breast; / like a child that is quieted is my soul."[16] We are being trained by our life as monks to have the childlike dependence on God that the gospel urges us toward by saying that we have to become as little

---

15. Matthew 5:3
16. Psalm 131:2; Rule of St. Benedict, Chapter 7, "On Humility"

children to enter the kingdom of heaven.[17] When we go to God at the end of our lives, we hope to be as we were at the beginning of our lives. We hope to have once more that trust we had as little infants absolutely dependent on our mothers, for the Lord has said to us, "Can a woman forget her sucking child, / that she should have no compassion on the son of her womb? / Even these may forget, / yet I will not forget you."[18]

17. Luke 18:16–17
18. Isaiah 49:15

Chapter Eighteen

THE SEA

Eternity, the Final Goal of My Life

Eternity is now enjoyed by those whose mortal remains lie in this cemetery. Although we may receive intuitions of eternity in our cloistered life, we do not know its fullness. Some things, however, can symbolize it for us. The sea is a specially potent symbol as it is traditionally associated with death. The Bible identifies the sea with the chaos and evil that can overwhelm people. But death is the gateway to eternity, and so the sea can also symbolize the unbounded life of eternity. Its scope reflects the infinity of the life beyond. To look at the sea is a way of contemplating eternity. Let us go down to the sea now. We are in the habit of walking down here often, if only to see that the sea is still there! For the monks who were here before us in old Quarr, however, the sea was important for their business, and to look at the sea is in a sense to be linked to them.

We turn right out of the cemetery and follow this path between fields till we come to the chestnut walk that leads us to the sea. I often go for a run down here. I hope that, by the mercy of God, my transition from this life to the peace of heaven will be equally speedy and that God's grace will have prepared me so that I do not need to wait for purification to be with him in eternity. At the end of this walk is the spot where I first read the Rule of St. Benedict. Actually, the spot is just beyond the end, because the

147

sea has eroded the coast. Probably it is now about where the tide is lapping at the shore. That is appropriate because it is through following this Rule that I hope to enter into eternity and be with God.

What that life is, we cannot say. Even possessing the life of the blessed, we cannot divulge this new, transformed identity. To the one who conquers, the Lord promises "a white stone, with a new name written on the stone which no one knows except him who receives it."[1] I hope to be like this little pebble here, picked up by the ocean of divinity, swept into the sea, and completely covered by the unsoundable depth of his bliss. Out here is the deepest part of the Solent. All the big ships come this way. Yet even the deepest sea cannot truly represent the depth of the mercy and love of God.

Many symbols speak of it, no symbol tells us of it as it is. When I look out of my window in the morning, I can see the sun rising over this sea. This speaks of it. The light as it dawns seems more encompassing even than the sea, yet I know that the sun will set and it will be night once more. It is an eternal dawn to which we look forward, an uncreated light. For the blessed, "night shall be no more; they need no light of lamp or sun, for the Lord God will be their light, and they shall reign for ever and ever."[2] That dawn comes to us through the resurrection of Christ, who endured the darkness of death. We sing of it when we sing the psalm we particularly associate with his resurrection, and proclaim, "This is the day which the LORD has made; / let us rejoice and be glad in it."[3]

Those moments in the cloister when time has faded away; that mysterious presence that is both in the church and in my heart, telling me that I am loved with a love that cannot be mea-

---

1. Revelation 2:17
2. Revelation 22:5
3. Psalm 118:24

sured; that intuition of a world beyond, which I have when I am reading what the saints wrote about life with God; that sense of One greater than any of us that comes to me in a moment shared with one of the brothers; that blessed hope whose seed has been sown in this place—all, all of this, is but the merest hint of the beatitude that God promises us, the beatitude of the eternal dawn. It is of this that my childhood spoke. The wonder and joy I felt then were but an anticipation of the wonder and joy that will be in my heart in that everlasting day. The holiday I then enjoyed with all the careless rapture of childhood was the merest hint of the enjoyment of the holiness of God to be enjoyed by every child of the eternal kingdom. Whitecliff Bay and Totland Bay, and all the beautiful vistas which this island offers, are only little tokens that God has given us to help us look forward to the bliss of gazing upon his uncreated beauty. This is the beauty for which we were made. This is the beauty that is hidden within the joys and sorrows of this world, its evanescent and partial manifestation. My life is dedicated to finding this beauty.

It is beauty unknown yet known: known in the still depths of the soul by the deep and subtle joy that radiates from it; known by the gestures of generous love that come from others; known by the beauty of nature, word, and worship. It is the beauty of the distant sky and yet it is the beauty of home. Just as the blue of the sky above us seems made for the green of the trees to our side here, so wonderfully do the colors match, so this heavenly beauty is made for us who live amidst the green of this earth. Green contains blue, and earth the seed of heaven, to which it tends.

And this beauty is still to find. The sea before us in one sense shows it to us. In another sense it is simply the place of our embarking for this voyage to the unknown, the sign of the death we must undergo before we can touch the blue beyond. The blue of the sea is murky and eddying; the blue of the beyond is crystal and still. To reach the horizon, the point of intersection of the timeless with time, we need to leave the earth we know and trustingly set sail for the passage to the unknown, going by a way we know not.

Yet we do not do this alone. This abbey is dedicated to Our Lady. Although for us at Quarr she is first of all Our Lady of Providence, she is also Our Lady, Star of the Sea. She is the one who can guide us through the waters of death. That plea, made so many times, "Pray for us sinners now and at the hour of our death," cannot go unanswered. Her presence is with us now; it will be with us at the hour of our death. She is our guide now, patient in her humility, loving us, praying for us; she will be our guide then, joyful in her love. She shows us now how to fulfil the deepest aspiration of the human heart, that yearning for heaven, not by the divisive pride and confusion that characterized the builders of the tower of Babel, but by humble receptiveness to the Spirit that heals division and brings peace. "Behold, I am the handmaid of the Lord; let it be to me according to your word,"[4] she says, and in saying this she represents the whole Church, all those who are journeying to their heavenly homeland, all those who want to die to self and, dying, enter life. She will show us at the hour of our death how to set the seal on that gift of self that is made in baptism and in monastic profession by giving back to God with a glad and generous heart that which we were but lent a while for our sojourn in this vale of soul making. She, our tainted nature's solitary boast, who has made that journey from earth to heaven, will be with us when we leave earth for our home where she is Queen.

That journey is given a poetic expression for me by one who lived on this island where I now live. Alfred Lord Tennyson walked the down now named for him where I walked with my family when I was on holiday here as a child. His poem "Crossing

---

4. Luke 1:38

the Bar" speaks of his own journey and of mine. It begins: "Sunset and evening star, / And one clear call for me!" Sunset is the end of the day but also the end of the day that ends, the passage to eternal light. The evening star reminds me of Mary, Star of the Sea, whose presence enlightens the darkness of death. The "one clear call for me" is at one and the same time the call of God to come to this monastery and the call of God to come to him at the end of my life on this earth. In God, there is no time. He is One and the love with which he calls me to be his friend in this place is undivided from the love with which he will (from my perspective) call me to himself when my earthly days are done: it is an eternal gift, made from all eternity. The "one clear call for me" is the ringing of the church bell here calling me to worship in this place; it is the summons to voyage across the waters of death; it is the celestial music inviting me to the harmony of heaven.

My prayer that this journey will be made in peace are expressed by the poem's words that immediately follow:

> And may there be no moaning of the bar,
>   When I put out to sea,
> But such a tide as moving seems asleep,
>   Too full for sound and foam,
> When that which drew from out the boundless deep
>   Turns again home.

"The bar" is the sandbank that causes the "sound and foam" when the tide is not full enough to cover it deeply. I pray the intrusion of earthbound and selfish concerns will not cause disturbance at my passage to eternity. Tennyson evokes Shakespeare's description of a life made meaningless by the pursuit of selfish ambition, one "full of sound and fury, signifying nothing."[5] My life as a monk is oriented toward avoiding this, now and at the hour of

---

5. *Macbeth*, Act 5, Scene 5, lines 27–28

my death. This is done by living from what is eternal rather than the shallow things of time, from the Creator rather than the creation. "Such a tide as moving seems asleep" suggests the power of God to put all things in motion while at the same time enjoying perfect rest himself. The depth of the sea at this tide symbolizes his eternity. From this "boundless deep" comes each human soul and thither, at the end of life, "turns again home."

From an earthly perspective, this homecoming appears to be going into the dark. Hence Tennyson says, "Twilight and evening bell, / And after that the dark!" The twilight is that final part of my life when my powers are fading; the evening bell is that summons to the Lord so often anticipated by our being called by a bell to the evening worship of Vespers. But in the perspective of heaven this going is an entry into light, for, as the psalmist sings, "even the darkness is not dark to thee, / the night is bright as the day; / for darkness is as light with thee."[6] That is why I want to make my own the poet's plea: "And may there be no sadness of farewell, / When I embark." I share the hope that he expresses in this final stanza of the poem:

> For though from out our bourne of Time and Place
>   The flood may bear me far,
> I hope to see my Pilot face to face
>   When I have crossed the bar.

"Our bourne of Time and Place" are the limits imposed on us by the particular circumstances of our life. They give an identity to our life but at the same time veil from us the glory of the world beyond. In entering eternity we leave behind these particular circumstances and enter into the fullness of eternal life. I pray "the flood" of that eternity will take me far beyond all that I have known. In it I will, please God, understand what everything that

---

6. Psalm 139:12

has been good in my life has been hinting at. My hope of seeing "my Pilot face to face" is my assurance that I will encounter Jesus (my Way), no longer veiled by sacrament and word but in his unmediated glory.

That will be a parting: a parting from my brothers here, a parting from the way of life that I know and love, but in another sense it will be a reuniting. I shall be reunited with God from whom I came and in that reuniting I shall know fully what here I have known only in part. "Then shall I know even as also I am known."[7] I shall know the fullness of the mystery that was concealed as well as expressed in our worship here and in all those moments when I have felt the presence of the One beyond. I shall know the One from whom all have their being and in whom all are held in being; and so, inwardly in him, I shall be with all those I have known and loved in this world, although outwardly there will be a parting.

And now the time is coming for you and me to part. Like that final parting, it is only outward and partial, for we are together in God, never more so than when we pray to him. So I ask you to pray for me as I do for you. Thank you for being with me, for listening as I have told the story of my life here. It is the story of one place only, and yet it is only in the particular that we ever find the universal. So, in a sense, one story is every story. I hope you have found in what I have said some echo of how God is calling you, for it cannot be that he who has lavished such love on his providential care of my undeserving self will fail to show his love in some special way for you also. Perhaps he will speak some word to your heart in this abbey that I love. Perhaps on this shore, which is at one and the same time, the shore of the Solent and the shore of eternity, he is waiting to speak to you of his undying love.

Or maybe God is waiting for you somewhere else.

---

7. 1 Corinthians 13:12 (King James Version)